Magdalena ⁝ Bak-Maier

Copyright 2019 MakeTimeCount

Disclaimer:

This book is written to help you recognize that you play an active role in your body's health and that integration of mind, heart, body and spirit supports well-being. The book is NOT intended as a substitute for medical advice particularly with respect to any symptoms that may require diagnosis and medical treatment. Body talk practice is meant to enhance and further support your chosen process - orthodox and/or alternative - of keeping yourself well.

# CONTENTS

## Preface — 11
My personal journey into living more in tune with my body — 13
Wherever we go, the mind comes too — 17
Self-care: the most important mindset and practice for the 21st Century — 19
Strong mind-body connection takes us a long way towards health, prosperity and wellbeing — 22
Being connected within is the foundation for living a good life — 25

## Introduction — 27
What is Body Talk? — 28
How I developed the Body Talk method — 29
Broken heart — broken body — 37
How to use this book — 39
What will you need? — 41
What Body Talk can do for you — 43

## Body Talk – Your Key to Greater Freedom — 47
Body Talk is a method and a process — 48
Is Body Talk the same as mindfulness? — 49
What can Body Talk do for me? — 51
How improving the body-mind connection can help you — 52
Ambition demands physical fitness — 54

| | |
|---|---|
| Our bodies and minds are intimately linked | 56 |
| Our bodies know things our minds don't | 59 |
| Systems within systems in need of balance and integration | 61 |

## The Body is a Major Superpower — 65

| | |
|---|---|
| Revealing your mind and body intelligences | 66 |
| Why modern life needs to practice Body Talk | 68 |
| The capacity for connection and disconnection always exists | 71 |
| The brain pays attention to what happens within us | 74 |
| Today's fast pace makes integration harder — unless we learn to pay attention | 75 |
| Your internal system is in constant update mode | 77 |
| Awareness builds with practice | 80 |
| The body is our superpower | 83 |
| Burnout happens because we stop paying conscious attention | 84 |
| A final word before we Body Talk… | 88 |

## Let's talk:
## 5 Activities to Kickstart a Conversation with Your Body — 89

| | |
|---|---|
| EXERCISE 1: Felt sense | 92 |
| EXERCISE 2: Body broadcast | 97 |
| EXERCISE 3 : Body map | 103 |
| EXERCISE 4: 7-day body dialogue | 107 |
| EXERCISE 5: Body timeline | 112 |
| Loving-kindness meditation | 120 |

## Let's Get Body Talking | 127
New friendship with your physical self starts here | 128
Body Talk method | 130
Body Talk: Your Step-by-step Guide | 132
The 9 key principles of the Body talk | 139
Quick recap! | 146

## Developing Your Practice Over 3 Months | 147
Creating your 3-month schedule | 148
Body map | 152
Note-taking Checklist | 153

## 3 Body Talk Options | 155
BODY TALK 1: When time is short | 156
BODY TALK 2: Standing body talk | 160
BODY TALK 3: In-depth body talk | 163
Frequently asked questions | 171

## 3 Month Review | 177
How to know if the Body Talk is helping me? | 178
Congratulations on getting reconnected | 181

## 5 Additional Activities to Deepen Internal Connection | 183
Introduction: Self-care is a vital practice and skill | 184
ACTIVITY 1: Hello me mirror exercise | 185
ACTIVITY 2: The hare & the tortoise | 190
ACTIVITY 3: Energy cylinders check | 196
ACTIVITY 4: Return Home | 200
ACTIVITY 5: Amplifying bliss | 207

| | |
|---|---|
| **Becoming a Master of Practice** | **213** |
| The science of body-centered health is growing | 214 |
| My top 10 Tips for a better you | 215 |
| Other Books by Magdalena | 224 |
| Ways to stay connected, engaged and more involved | 225 |
| Help us spread integration work | 227 |
| **About** | **229** |
| Magdalena Bak-Maier | 230 |
| What is integration? | 231 |
| How the work develops and who I share it with | 233 |
| Make Time Count | 235 |
| Acknowledgements | 237 |

For those who want to be healthy and free to live their best life

"It is easier to suffer than to heal."
Bert Hellinger

Many of us
communicate
way too much with
our mind
and
far too little
with
our
bodies and hearts
or the voice of the
spirit.

This book aims to
help you
change this dynamic
so you can return
to a far more
balanced,
integrated,
more effective
and
happy
you.

## Preface

*"I journey for and with my clients.
I go where they go. I see what they see.
I am with them no matter what.
I also travel life on my own behalf.
To experience it. To taste its richness.
To discover its depths and to simply have an experience I can call my own."*
Magdalena Bak-Maier, Neuroscientist, integration pioneer, and healer

My work has always chosen me. It seems to come calling, asking me to be curious, to experiment and to discover things that will serve others. My Body Talk method came out of one such calling. I'd like to share with you a simple tool that will rekindle a conversation with your physical body, a conversation that will last a lifetime and support you to live your best, most authentic life. Welcome to my simple, science-backed Body Talk method.

I have found that having a respectful dialogue with my body is incredibly useful for healing past trauma, working through conflicts between my emotions and thoughts and being mindfully tuned into my physical body as a source of wisdom. This work has drastically improved they way I look after myself: my self-care. I have evolved this practice for close to 20 years. In the process, my sense of empowerment and my physical, emotional and mental wellbeing have drastically improved. The practice has also helped me become a better coach.

My client work and retreats show incredible results that attest to the transformative power when the whole of your being, not just your brain (which for most of us loves to dominate) has a stake in your present and future. My Body Talk is a great method for helping to reconnect within. I've share the Body Talk practice with my coaching clients and have seen ambitious, passionate individuals, who often spend too much time in their own mind, become more content and at the same time highly successful because they learn to reconnect with their true feelings, longings, values and their essence. I have watched and helped them learn to hear their body speak. I know the same is possible for everyone.

When we are operating in harmony with our body, we simply feel more joined-up and at home in ourselves. We begin to feel as though the stars are aligned and we're on the right track, because we are truly listening to what our whole self needs. I'm glad you're here.

*Magdalena Bak Maier*

## My personal journey into living more in tune with my body

*"Neuroscience research shows that the only way we can change the way we feel is by becoming aware of our inner experience and learning to befriend what is going inside ourselves."*
Bessel A. van der Kolk, Clinician, leading researcher and teacher in the area of post-traumatic stress

I remember becoming acutely aware of my physical body as a teenager. I recall the sense of awe and joy I experienced dancing on my rollerblades in the park; my body felt free and perfectly aligned with what I felt inside. I was totally in tune with myself. The first memory of feeling this way takes me back to being about eight years old, riding my bike feeling free through the countryside of rural Poland where I was born. I moved to America when I was twelve. Having to move countries and find my place in a new school, new neighborhood and new culture was highly stressful. Having to learn to speak English when you're no longer a little child was also not easy. My hard-working parents were often not skilled at supporting me through these stressful events.

I went through cycles of weight gain and weight loss – I would comfort eat without realizing it, only to feel regret for not being the skinny teen so often portrayed in American advertising. I studied and worked hard, desperate to escape my circumstances and find a way to break out. This meant having a part-time job to have my own pocket money as well as staying on top of my schoolwork and home responsibilities. I did not know this at the time, but I was in effect self-parenting and developing maturity far beyond my years as a way to simply survive. Having no other family near me, I had no one to go to other than a self-help book when I felt scared. I did not feel my parents could or would understand. I tried to tell them how I felt, but failed.

When I was unhappy, I felt disconnected from my physical body and myself. I began to use productivity as a means of coping. If I was busy studying, working or doing something of value, I did not have to face how lonely I felt. I desired to be super slim and fit; in my mind this was the ideal image for high school and college. However, my mental and emotional struggles kept drawing me back to feeling unmotivated to exercise, seeking comfort in eating and proving myself in any arena I could. When I discovered rollerblades and began to dance on them while listening to music on my headphones, I finally found a way to connect my feelings with my body and give them a creative expression.

But my most significant experience of the mind-body connection came during my PhD in developmental neuroscience at Caltech – California Institute of Technology. It proved the catalyst for my life-long quest to understand how the mind and body interact and what this means for our performance, happiness and health.

All PhDs are hard work. You're required to set out and independently create new knowledge in your chosen field. It's a big responsibility and a massive quest. Some students receive a great deal of hand-holding but this was not the case at Caltech. The institution is world-renowned for attracting and training world-class scientists including Albert Einstein, Stephen Hawking, Linus Pauling, Richard Feynman, Charles Richter, David Baltimore, and many others. You were expected to think for yourself; the culture was very much "sink or swim". The first year was very tough physically, emotionally and intellectually. The place was also male-dominated. I worked long hours needing to quickly master many techniques, come to grips with existing knowledge, master state of the art techniques, design

BODY TALK

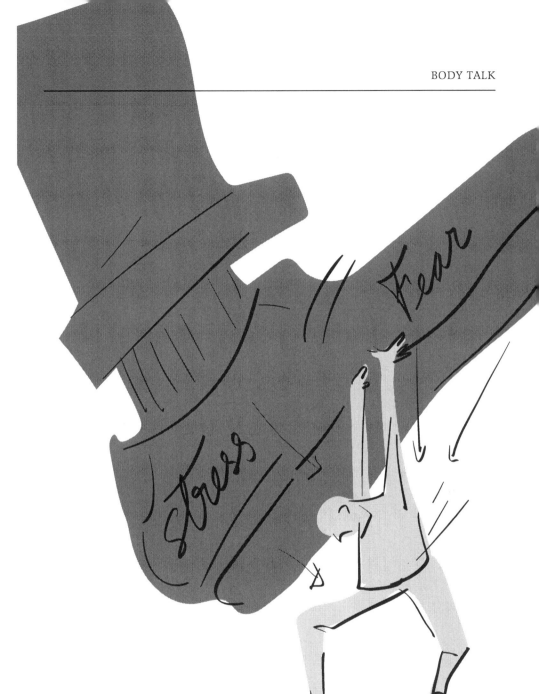

experiments and learn to operate complex imaging microscopes. I had to prove my independence and in effect earn my place in the lab in less than a year.

The incredible stress of needing to publish in high impact journals affected me to my core. Initially I was overcome with fear of surviving, fear of not fitting in, fear of being not good enough, and in the end even fear of succeeding. I began to have panic attacks and I remember feeling utter frustration, that my body was betraying me. Anxiety, tiredness, stress, the constant culture of competition and criticism all took their toll in the form of chronic stress from high pressure work without appropriate emotional support.

The stress I was under built up to such a degree that it took my body to tell me, in the most physical way with cold sweats, uncontrollable shaking, heart palpitations, muscle weakness, hallucinations and breathlessness that this was not the way to succeed! On one occasion, I ended up in the emergency unit with a suspected heart attack, which the ER crew likened to the results of a drug overdose. But it wasn't drugs. It was adrenaline from intolerable levels of stress. Enough was enough.

## Wherever we go, the mind comes too

With the help of a counselor and an inspirational yoga teacher, the panic attacks subsided. Whilst I tried to offset my stress with weekend trips away into nature, a life drawing class and lots of cooking to relax me, what I found was that wherever you go, your mind follows. And if this mind is troubled and deeply scared, if it has incessant worries and constant thoughts you can't shut off, you're in perpetual hell. In the end, the things that set me on the road to recovery were those that help the mind reconnect with the security of unconditional love: a pet dog, the love and support from my then boyfriend and later husband, and learning to switch off with yoga and meditation. I worked through my internal turmoil with a daily journaling practice and numerous self-care rituals such as lighting a candle or playing music from nature or simply showing up to the gym on a daily basis for half an hour to work off my angsts, frustrations, conflicts and fears, converting them to sweat.

These practices made me feel good – there was no goal or endgame other than progressively feeling more balanced, stronger and more resilient. I started to find a new sense of joy and aliveness, a joy that I hadn't experienced since I was a teenager dancing on those rollerblades feeling free. Up to this point, my unspoken agreement with my physical body was that it was there to do my bidding, to be pushed or ignored. I certainly didn't treat it the way you would treat a friend or someone who you want on your side. My PhD days gave me a new appreciation for how powerful an ally or foe the body can be. Learning to listen to it, work within its limits as well as to connect mind and body helped me sleep better, be more productive and focused. I learned to work and live in a far more inspired way. It also helped me to stay kind to others when often such pressure brings out the worst aspects of ourselves.

*17*

## PREFACE

The reason these practices were so powerful, I discovered, was because they brought my mind, heart, body and spirit together into better alignment. No longer was my mind running the show and bullying the other parts of me into submission. Such alignment is known in science as 'integration'- a way to ensure that all key elements of something are included. The Body Talk method I describe in this book will help you to live a more integrated and thus healthier life.

Body Talk involves spending regular time paying attention to yourself - your whole self, not just your thoughts. Often, we listen only to what our mind is telling us, forgetting that the body holds vital wisdom too or that we have feelings. Body Talk teaches you a way of tapping into a source of wisdom you may have forgotten that you posses. In the process, it will help you become calmer, more grounded, wiser and far more resourceful.

## Self-care: the most important mindset and practice for the 21st Century

I care deeply about helping people to thrive and I know from my own experience as well as my scientific work that it all starts with self-care. Freeing the body of stressors and pain requires a proactive and holistic approach to health that is increasingly accepted by Western medicine. This starts with how we care for our mental, emotional, physical and spiritual wellbeing as imbalance in any of them has holistic consequences for the total being.

In 2005, the UK Department of Health elevated self-care and assigned everyone responsibility for it. "Self-care is a part of daily living. It is the care taken by individuals towards their own health and wellbeing, and includes the care extended to their children, family, friends and others in neighbourhoods and local communities." In a nutshell self-care is a conscious choice. It is thus rooted in a mind-set of personal responsibility and positive regard towards self. Self-care is proactive and preventive rather than reactive. Today it is the biggest weapon against the number one epidemic: stress!

Over the last few years, self-care has been increasingly seen as a key building block in patient-centered health services. Taking an active role in self-care results in better patient outcomes, better use of medical intervention and strengthens social care bonds. In other words the more we approach ourselves and each other with love and care, the better we recover and heal.

The International Self-Care Foundation (http://isfglobal.org), a UK-based registered charity focused uniquely on the strategic worldwide promotion and development of a self-care and healthy lifestyles, defines self-care as practical, person-cantered set of activities that we should all be doing to maintain our health, wellness and wellbeing.

1. Health literacy: Knowing one's options medical or otherwise.

2. Self-awareness. Acknowledging one's physical, emotional, social, spiritual, and professional needs.

3. Physical activity. Exercise and movement being recognised as a crucial activity to boost positive brain chemistry and help improve overall physical and emotional health.

4. Healthy eating. A deliberate choice to eat a nutritious and healthy diet.

5. Risk mitigation. Taking care to lower existing risks where possible.

6. Good hygiene. Taking care of one's body.

7. Rational use of medicine and therapies.

When it comes to Body Talk and your wellbeing, this means:

1. Understanding that your mind, heart, body and spirit create one integrated self.

2. Developing and/or strengthening your skills of working with your integrated self.

3. Paying attention to your physical body as a vital source of information about how you are.

4. Making a deliberate choice to listen to your body.

5. Commitment to looking after yourself.

6. Finding a way to balance what's important to each part of you and what it needs to be well.

7. Seeking additional help as needed.

PREFACE

# Strong mind-body connection takes us a long way towards health, prosperity and wellbeing

As a diabetic, I have seen first-hand the benefits of robust self-care in the way I have managed and even improved my condition. This book will show you how you too can improve your life, by connecting more to your physical body.

On International Women's Day 2018, my editor, the talented yoga practitioner and journalist Victoria Woodhall, named me one of the top 10 inspirational women in wellness on wellness and beauty platform Getthegloss.com. She credited me with introducing the term 'self-care' into mainstream conversation about productivity. My book *The Get Productive Grid* talks about how vital self-care is to doing well both at work and in your career. My Body Talk method deepens this message and offers many practical tools for self-care.

Our bodies are key players in the way we look after ourselves and we ignore them at our peril, as I know both from personal experience and as a top performance coach. I've observed time and again that the people who recognise the importance of the body are those who achieve their full potential and who sustain their performance over time.

Dr. Alan Goldberg is a Sports Performance Consultant and international expert in peak sports performance for athletes from junior level to Olympians. He recommends a holistic approach to getting to the top and staying there. While learning to stay focused and disciplined is key, all athletes have to learn to rest and balance their rigorous training, he says. Secondly, however successful they are, the best athletes always remember that they are a human being first and an athlete second. In other words, who they are is much more than what they do or the goals they set for themselves. I must admit that working primarily with top performers in research and creative industries I apply the same principles to them.

I have also seen countless clients overlook this vital element. They either choose or habitually fall into patterns of overworking, sleep deprivation, chronic stress, lack of movement and exercise, shallow breathing, poor diet, weight gain, substance abuse, unhealthy addictions and physical neglect of their body. Once they feel stress, their performance suffers and they become more frustrated. They may have insomnia and panic attacks, lose confidence and self-esteem, experience inner emptiness and lose their love for life. A good number of clients will come to my practice when they get to that stage and are ready to finally take steps to reframe their approach to life. Some have been trapped in an unhelpful stress cycle for years before they seek help. All this time they have been exposed to negative mental, emotional and physical stress. The longer such chronic stress continues, the more the person risks stress-related illnesses such as autoimmune conditions. Without counter measures, some will end up with serious depression, chronic fatigue and even nervous breakdown. What is so perplexing is that most of these people achieve great results for others and yet pay the ultimate personal price with their health and personal wellbeing.

But it doesn't have to be this way. A simple habit of regularly checking in with our body is one the most powerful ways to reconnect with your whole self and thrive. Our body loves a regular 'how are you really?' catch-up - in the same way that we might ring our mother weekly and ask her whether she needs anything or check in with our closest friends. Our body is a better friend to us and more likely to impart those nuggets of wisdom when we're in regular contact and when we're listening. This book will show you how to do that

PREFACE

no matter how busy you are so you can discover the magic of connection for yourself.

## Being connected within is the foundation for living a good life

Being connected with our bodies helps us create greater stability, grounding and centeredness. A strong mind-body connection is foundational to living a good life because we experience life and act in it with the help of our bodies. It is key to greater presence, leadership, sense of who we are and what our purpose is, sense of wellness, fulfilment and achievement of results. The rewards are greater confidence and self-regard, increased resilience and the feeling of being grounded – all of which are vital for leadership in our complex times.

As you put Body Talk into action in your life, your connection with your body will deepen, allowing you to discover a new source of power and strength. I hope that you discover the beauty, potential and utter marvel of your reconnected self and the ways in which it can serve your life and others.

INTRODUCTION

INTRODUCTION

INTRODUCTION

## What is Body Talk?

- Body Talk is a practice that helps you connect your physical body with your mind, heart and spirit.

- It is achieved through placing deliberate attention on different parts of your body in order to listen to its perspective, intelligence and truth.

- Having this dialogue regularly helps cultivate a deeply respectful connection between mind and body, which can support what you want to create in the world and get the best out of who you are.

- You are first and foremost your body. Distanced from it, you cease to 'feel' life. Without it, you cease to exist.

- Body Talk will help you become more whole, more integrated and it will benefit your physical, mental, emotional and spiritual health.

- The practice takes as little as three minutes and I recommend a three-month learning phase

## How I developed the Body Talk method

The Body Talk comes from my personal adventure in developing a mindful conversation with my own body over the last 20 years. I was a stressed and anxious PhD student who had a wakeup call when panic attacks were so severe I ended up in a hospital. When I was young I did not pay much attention to tiredness and I'd use caffeine and sugar to power through. I would grant my body occasional rest by having long 10 to 12 hour sleeps or taking the occasional escape into nature. I would knowingly and wilfully push it beyond its limits the rest of the time staying up late, working too many hours, having little play time and then playing too hard. It wasn't a fair exchange, in fact it was pure arrogance – I was taking my body for granted. What I did well, though, was to stick with a regular daily journaling practice.

### Writing things down

My journaling practice began when I was around 12 years old when I began to keep a diary. I wrote about my experiences and how they made me feel, what I wanted to create and accomplish and what I struggled with. Having my own safe space to face my full experience of life was incredibly helpful as a way of saying what I often would not dare to say out loud. The pages listened without dismissing my feelings. If I wanted to write pages, I could and there was no one to stop me. If I wanted to write just a single sentence, I could. Over time, I would use my diary to write down inspirational quotes, summaries of passages and ideas I came across in books and exhibitions. I even used it as a canvas to brainstorm ideas.

Open and always welcoming, journals became my best friend.

Allowing me to work through things in my own way and helping me address the needs of my heart, spirit and my body. The more I wrote

*29*

## INTRODUCTION

the more I noticed how helpful it was to do that on a regular basis. Many years later I came across a best-selling book by Julia Cameron entitled *The Artist's Way*. In it the author introduces a practice called the morning pages in which you write few pages of stream of consciousness truth first thing in the morning every day. It turned out I had invented my own version.

Writing about your feelings helps the mind make sense of emotional experiences. Studies done by Prof Matthew Lieberman, a psychologist at the University of California, Los Angeles show that giving feelings an expression – whether that's through talking about them, naming them or writing about them – helps us feel better[1].

Dr Lieberman and his team have used brain-imaging studies to show how anger and sadness lessen when the mind processes emotions. In one study, volunteers were shown images of faces with different facial expressions. Underneath each picture was a choice of a label and the volunteer had to choose between 'angry' or 'fearful'. As a control, volunteers were also given the same image with labels that simply denoted the gender of the person in the picture. Volunteers who were shown the word 'angry' had reduced levels of activation in a part of the brain called the amygdala, which is involved in controlling emotions, especially fear and its intensity. They also noted more activity int the right ventro-lateral prefrontal cortex (VLPC), a part of the brain involved in higher-level processing when we reappraise a situation (especially a negative stimulus) in order to minimize its emotional impact. Lieberman also showed that putting feelings into words activates a higher cortical area that is able to dampen an activated amygdala when we're frightened or scared.

---

1  Lieberman, M. D., Eisenberger, N. I., Crockett, M. J., Tom, S. M., Pfeifer, J. H., & Way, B. M. (2007). Putting Feelings Into Words. *Psychological Science*, 18(5), 421–428. https://doi.org/10.1111/j.1467-9280.2007.01916.x

Some of the participants also completed a survey on mindfulness, the technique of paying conscious attention to your emotions, thoughts and body sensations in the present without judgment. A key goal in mindfulness practice is to simply observe something without needing to react. Let's say you're going to tune into your body and notice that your feet feel cold. That would be an example of a mindful observation. You become aware of the feeling and name the sensation. We do the same when we admit we feel happy, sad or angry. What Dr Lieberman and his colleagues showed was that people with higher scores on the mindfulness questionnaire had more activation in the prefrontal cortex in general, and in the right VLPC. Thus, by naming emotions we stop them from hijacking our brain.

One researcher who has studied the health benefits of expressive writing is Dr James W. Pennebaker, American social psychologist working at the University of Texas, Austin. According to Dr Pennebaker, thinking about an emotionally charged experience that affects us forces us to organise thoughts and create meaning from it[2][3][4]. James Pennebaker's studies build on the work of psychotherapist and journal therapy pioneer, Kathleen Adams[5]. They affirm the role of writing about our emotional problems as an effective way towards recovery and maintaining wellbeing.

---

2  Pennebaker J. W., & Evans J. (2014). Expressive writing: Words that heal. Enumclaw, WA : Idyll Arbor, Inc.
3  Pennebaker, J. W., & Smyth, F. J. (2016). Opening up by writing it down: the healing power of expressive writing (3rd ed.). New York, NY: Guilford.
4  Pennebaker, J. W. (2018). Expressive Writing in Psychological Science. Perspectives on Psychological Science, 13(2), 226–229. https://doi.org/10.1177/1745691617707315 https://doi.org/10.1177/1745691617707315
5  Adams, K. (2004). Scribing the Soul: Essays in Journal Therapy. Wheat Ridge, CO, USA: Center for Journal Therapy. Also see an interview with Adams for Psychology Today https://www.psychologytoday.com/intl/blog/ethical-wisdom/201401/journal-the-self-interview-kathleen-adams

INTRODUCTION

You will not have to look very far to find studies that show the benefits of writing as therapy to deal with grief and loss, trauma and many health conditions. What was true for me, as my journaling practice grew, was this: whether it was morning or evening, or middle of the day, I would simply resolve to sit and write down how I was really feeling, being truthful to my experience. Part of this included making observations and notes about how my body felt as a physical entity. Sometimes I would just write "My shoulders ache!" or "another horrible headache!"

Then one day my curious mind simply asked the question "How do other parts feel?" To cheer myself up, I would ask, "Which part of my body is *not* hurting or feeling fatigued?" As I turned my awareness inwards, an answer would come from my wiggling toes or a feeling that my hands were keen to get creative. Sometimes I would notice a pleasant vortex of energy swirling in my chest even though my shoulders and neck muscles were screaming in pain. This was the start of my Body Talk practice. But for a long time I would simply use my rational mind to speak for my body. For example, I would look at my feet and say "My toes could use a pedicure" which was true and logical or "I'd love my belly to disappear" or "My boobs are big again, I must have put on weight."

Notice how these statements were nothing more than evaluations and a way of trying to problem-solve my body as if it was an object. A more mindful true response when one does Body Talk is to suspend what the mind thinks and simple be present to what emerges from the body. For example, when really listening to my toes they may have said something like "We want to experience being touched." Or the belly may say "Go dancing Mag!"

In a sense, at the beginning I was really only paying lip service to my body. It would be a long time before I really caught on to where the truthful and useful answers were coming from. With each practice, something shifted. Gradually I opened my mind and heart to the idea of asking my body how it felt and what it needed, and of using my mind to simply listen with love and respect to what arose from my body. Looking back at my journals, I can see a deliberate practice of deep listening to my body emerged after five years.

## Drawing a body map

After completing my PhD I moved to the United Kingdom and discovered sculpture. When I didn't have time to indulge my hobby, I'd draw my body inspired by Picasso's simple black lines and fast inspirational sketches. The drawings became part of my journaling practice and Body Talk method. Rather than just writing about body parts and what they told me or asked me for, I would draw a figure

INTRODUCTION

without putting much thought to it as a map to record my Body Talk. In fact, many of the drawings you will encounter in this book are based on my drawings. When I looked back over my journals, all of my early figures were standing. It took about eight years before one of my drawings sat down. I believe this to be a highly significant and very accurate depiction of how I was: busy whilst my mind ran ahead trying to dominate. Some had big feet and others long necks. Some had no toes but resembled more abstract forms that corresponded to general human body geography. It is safe to say that I'm not an artist and yet each drawing was incredibly unique and somehow beautiful because I allowed it to simply flow out of me, without thought, pause or much contemplation. I felt its energy, my hand converted it into a line on a page and I began to trust that line implicitly.

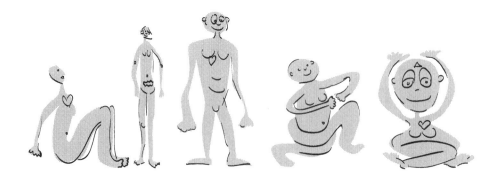

Back then I did not even think to research whether drawing could be effective for managing stress. Now as a practitioner I am far more aware of how effective drawing is in counseling and psychotherapy work with both children and adults. As a coach, I have seen the incredible power of drawings to create clarity, help illustrate what may be difficult to say and aid many people in expressing their true state[6]. One example is a stick figure drawing I ask clients to make to capture how things are now and how they would like them to be.

I call it the 2-minute sketch. The body map drawing aided my note taking. I simply followed what my hand felt was instinctively right for me. Often I was unaware of what the body map would look like until it appeared on the page. Attuning to an inner knowing, the body map gave my practice additional structure and a map for exploring my body more systematically.

I'd long been a fan of guided meditation ever since a career counsellor introduced me to it as an undergraduate. I volunteered at the counseling center as a student and developed a fruitful relationship with one of the staff members; a Native American descendant and a very spiritual person. A number of times, she would help me manage my stress and anxiety by practicing guided visualisations with me. Sometimes she would invite me to simply close my eyes and allow visions to come into my mind as if my own spirit or other spirits were there to guide and support me. She taught me how to breathe and stay in meditation. Whilst I did not know this at the time, in many ways, she was a conduit to my discovery of my innate ability to attune to, and work with, energy and spirit. Over the years I retained, adopted and

---

6   I find the Mood Cards pack created by Andrea Harrn and Stacey Siddons very helpful in my 1:1 work.

evolved these practices – meditation, mindfulness, guided visualisation, journaling and drawing – to form the basis of my Body Talk.

These days I have a highly intentional, respectful and loving dialogue with my body as friend and wise counsel. I see my body as a home for my mind, heart and spirit. My body knows my thoughts and feelings. It has been with me through every experience. My body remembers or has a felt sense of things in a way that is far richer than a simple factual memory. It is able to furnish me with insight, wisdom and uncannily astute observations; all with my total wellbeing in mind. If a specific part of my body makes an observation or logs a request – for example it may ask me to take myself to the seaside, or to walk barefoot in dewy grass – I listen.

I have found a new relationship between my mind and my body. One where the mind no longer judges or speaks on behalf of the body but instead listens, hears and does its best to honor the requests it makes. My Body Talk practice contains drawings, observations, and tick boxes allowing me to review what happening in the present and what my body still requires. I love going back over previous body map drawings and notes and ticking requests off as having been delivered. If I listen, it speaks. If I neglect it, it goes silent.

My drawings over the last 15 years make a fascinating record of mind-body conversations. They show me a timeline of myself in the world and a means of keeping track of the requests my body has made. They help me see and appreciate how the combined intelligence of my spirit supports me in self-realising my potential. I also get to see how I've helped my body get what it needed and where I still neglect it. It is clear that those requests are also what I needed as a person in order to perform well, be happy and healthy.

## Broken heart — broken body

Eight years ago, my body had perhaps its most important message for me. I split up with my husband which shattered my world. It was true trauma. At the same time, I fell in love with someone else but the relationship was not meant to be. Over this time period, I had no time for Body Talk at all. My life was dominated by one giant emotional rollercoaster while successfully maintaining a high-performance job and an external façade that I was OK. I was anything but!

The emotional stress this time was far worse than the psychological stress my PhD demanded. I felt a number of times as if I was going to die. As I had used sugar to cope with stress through childhood traumas, I was now using sugar again - and caffeine. So many times, I felt the urge to smoke and drink and if it were not for a good friend and professional counselor, who pointed out that I was choosing to self-harm, I would no doubt have given into it. But instead, I had her support. It proved a critical lifeline. When I spoke to her about how I felt, I noticed my body tension easing. She listened patiently without judgment, affirmed my needs and feelings, helping me be with what was happening to me. I also resumed my journaling and Body Talk to help me cope.

I was diagnosed with Type 1 diabetes in 2012 at the age of 36. Being an autoimmune condition, the illness likely began earlier and coincided with the slow death of my marriage and coming to terms with my sexuality as a gay woman. My illness humbled my ego and strengthened my spirit. I developed a deep appreciation, love and compassion for my physical body. I began to see my mind, heart, body and spirit working together as a pure miracle. At the core of it was my body. My body had an incredible power and wisdom that I was greatly underestimating.

INTRODUCTION

Many of us have limitations imposed on us by our bodies, whether that's through illness or injury, but in my experience Body Talk can help lessen those frustrations. It can help us flip self-loathing and fear that compromise health and erode happiness. Integration helps stop harmful denial in its tracks. Instead, this practice makes space for compassion and healing to occur. Our bodies have much wisdom to impart if we show up and listen. For example, my Body Talk, along with regular blood sugar readings, show me that my biggest source of sugar highs coincide with emotional and psychological stresses. My diabetes resides in my body, but my mind influences it. My body is highly sensitive to what I think and how my mind perceives threat. This has major consequences for my physiology. Thus, my body is my litmus paper.

My Body Talk method has helped me reconnect with my body in a highly empowering way. I use it to detect when I push too hard and as counsel to tell me what I need to do instead. In spite of my condition, my body does not feel like an adversary. It is my closest ally. I wish the same to be true for you.

## How to use this book

This book begins with activities, which will set you up for the Body Talk process. Please work through the book in sequence. The activities will help you do the following:

1. Establish a starting point to your mind-body connection (Pg 89)

2. Guide you through the Body Talk practice (Pg 127)

3. Help you develop your practice and shape it into your own internal reconnection work (Pg 183)

The invitation in this book is for you to get to know your body. Knowing something does not automatically change our life until we integrate new information into our existing ways of being. What we discover and practice can then become part of what we do on a regular basis. The late yoga master and founder of Ashtanga Yoga Sri K Pattabhi Jois was often asked to explain the mysteries of yoga by students who wanted to know why it worked. His reply was always, 'Practice and all is coming.'

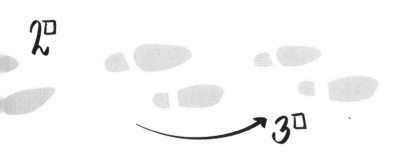

INTRODUCTION

Like Pattabhi Jois, I would encourage you simply to spend a few minutes a day doing the Body Talk and to experience its effects ripple through your daily life. Make it a habit, and 'all will come'.

## What will you need?

The Body Talk can be carried out almost anywhere so long as you're alone and can remain undisturbed. I have performed the exercise on a beach, sitting on a bench in a city park, and once in a cathedral. Most often however, I Body Talk on my bed sitting up with my journal or in a living room sitting on the sofa. Sometimes I'll do the practice in my garden. What's key is that you're in a peaceful and pleasant surrounding that allows you to focus on yourself.

Body Talk practice can be given as much or as little time as you can spare, but you'll usually need a minimum of 5 minutes for a very short version and about 20 to 30 minutes for a fuller exercise. With time, you will become quicker at it. I sometimes find that I am called to spend quality time with my body in sacred dialogue – a process I give around 40 min.

Initially, you might want to follow my guided Body Talk audio. You will find the recordings at www.maketimecount.com/bodytalk/media. However, you'll soon pick up the technique and not require my help.

Have a journal to hand in order to note what comes up and in which to draw a body map if you wish. Having a dedicated journal is a nice way to look at how you are progressing. I date my Body Talk entries.

Bring a clear intention to simply be present with your body and listen without expectations. A deep presence and communion with the body underpin effective Body Talk practice. Imagine meeting an old friend and simply being with them without attachment to time or specific outcome other than having a curiosity about what's going on with them.

## INTRODUCTION

If Body Talk sounds odd to you at first, it may be your rational mind defending itself from a practice that is going against its usual dominance. Often people ask me "what do you mean listen to your body speak. Is it not the mind that is speaking?" As you will find only by practicing, the mind often starts off this way, but you will soon discern its opinions, views and judgments and be able to spot them for what they are: 'mind speak'. When the body speaks, there's an intuitive sense of awareness that arises from the body or specific body part. In Body Talk, it is this greater knowing that the mind picks up and communicates to you in a form of awareness. This is what we want to capture in Body Talk.

## What Body Talk can do for you

I called my company Make Time Count because I believe life to be precious. It is easy to drift only to wake and come to the painful realization that time has slipped away and you could have been living a more present life. Often this can happen when the mind is chasing goals and we get caught living our lives from the neck up. By focusing so much on what's coming next, we divert our attention from the present and, along with it, the joy and possibility of the moment we're in.

With my integration work, I recognise and celebrate the preciousness of life. My mission is to help my clients become fully present in life with the whole of their being, while still having and achieving their goals. My own experience of ignoring my body's needs is not unusual, nor is the constant sense of feeling I need to choose between what

## INTRODUCTION

my heart and mind want. I see it all around me. Allow me to help you reconnect with your body to harness even greater power within yourself. By reconnecting your inner truth through the body, you will surface your deepest needs, longings, and internal conflicts that must come to the surface where your total self – mind, heart, body and spirit – can work on them.

What's holding you back in life and work?

Do any of these apply to you? If so, then Body Talk is for you.

- Your body seems to let you down by feeling tired, having unexplained symptoms, lack of sleep and generally not supporting you in the pursuit of your goals.

- You have to really push yourself to achieve what you want.

- You get sick easily, have pains and health problems.

- You feel disconnected from your body, as if you were watching yourself from afar, going through your daily experiences.

- You think too much.

- You often feel torn between what your heart and mind want and what is good for you.

- You feel lost and disconnected from life and from yourself.

What do you want more of?

Body Talk is for you personally or for your clients, if you're a coach or counselor, if you wish to achieve more of the following:

- A greater connection with your body.
- Greater resilience and internal calm.
- Feeling more grounded and stable in life.
- Creating a satisfying life that supports physical health.
- Feeling stronger and more content in the body.
- Having a healthier body.
- Greater presence and personal power.
- Stronger embodied leadership.
- Higher levels of productivity.
- Deeper and more meaningful connection with life.
- Intimate connection with other people and oneself.

# Body Talk
# – Your Key to
# Greater Freedom

## Body Talk is a method and a process

Body Talk is a method for connecting with your body through deliberate and intentional dialogue. It is also a process. Repeated over time Body Talk practice will help you reconnect mind, heart, body and spirit. Body Talk involves making time to listen to what your body has to tell you about what is going on with you. The purpose is to hear deeper truths - body wisdom - that emanate from places other than your ego.

Body wisdom reflects our greater spirit: our emotional state and the things our minds may be suppressing or simply not wanting to acknowledge. For example, I may know I have chest pain, which my mind tells me is stress and anxiety. However, a Body Talk might bring up a completely different answer. It may say that the pain is actually a physical manifestation of a long-standing conflict with a parent. Only I will know whether what surfaces feels true even if my mind may want to block it and what I wish to do about it.

The vital aspect of the Body Talk practice is that I now have an insight and a choice to examine this new information and act upon it. For example, if I visit the doctor and get my health checked out, it may appear that there is nothing physically wrong with me and yet I may continue to feel otherwise. Instead, if I manage to address the relationship with my parent, I may find that the physical symptoms also lessen or disappear. In this way, Body Talk work is sacred and soulful work that yields powerful and profound results.

## Is Body Talk the same as mindfulness?

Mindfulness practices emphasize being in the present moment. We are encouraged to notice how our minds wander back and forth in time and we try to develop the skill of noticing this behaviour while returning our attention to the present moment without judgment.

Body Talk is certainly a mindful practice, but it is a bit different. In Body Talk we are deploying our attention in a different way. We are asking the mind to pay attention to our bodies and to make conscious links between the information it is given by the body so it can relate this sense to what else it knows about us. Body Talk harnesses the mind's ability to link our past and present. Whilst mindfulness attempts to anchor us to the present, Body Talk practice captures information from the present about what the body may have experienced in the past. Our goal is to maintain our awareness of what arises whilst also linking that awareness with a larger context of our experience. Thus, rather than working to delay the mind, in Body Talk we assign the mind a function to help us understand what our body is telling us, reconnect our emotions with logic and help our spirit blossom.

Body Talk invites you to connect with your inner knowing and felt sense to hear what is true for your embodied self. We ask and receive this truth. This in turn creates an easing that occurs at different levels: physical, mental, emotional and spiritual. Body map drawings and diary practice are used to support the dialogue process and we actively seek to engage the mind's key function rather than trying to disconnect from it.

To return to the earlier example, if my heart hurts and the awareness that I receive is that this discomfort is connected with my father, my mind will be able to evaluate whether this is probable or not. Whilst the goal of many meditations is to free ourselves from thoughts, here we focus on balancing their usual dominance with greater wisdom and awareness from a different source: our body. Doing this can give us a much fuller picture of who we really are and what we need.

Body Talk combines three elements: the body scan - a well-known meditation practice - with elements of a focusing method developed by the American psychologist and philosopher Eugene Gendlin and finally art therapy. Body scan meditations use physical sensations and visualizations to root the mind in the physical body and to experience how the body feels in the present moment. Body scan meditation has been researched and proven to aid wellbeing, help decrease physical discomfort and pain, assist with the management of anxiety and many pain conditions, and reduce stress levels. Focusing, meanwhile helps people open up to their inner world of feelings, intuition and experience in a way that improves their empathy and listening. Drawings help give expression to ideas, feelings and experiences that can be difficult to verbalise. As drawing and writing tap different parts of the brain, Body Talk helps connect more brain regions and circuits.

## What can Body Talk do for me?

We're going to re-engage you with your body. For many of us, our body is like the student in class who keeps putting their hand up, but whom the teacher (the mind) continually ignores. This student has valuable insights to bring to the lesson and could even teach the teacher a thing or two, but because they are not being asked to contribute, they switch off. The result is that everyone loses out.

With this practice, we're going to change that conversation. We will recruit your body as an equal partner in our life's mission. As you will discover within the pages of this book,

- mindfulness practices

- love and safety in relationships

- the power of self-care

positively impact our health and wellbeing. Reconnecting with ourselves and each other by harnessing mind, heart and body supports us in staying resilient, healthy and doing well. And yet, when it comes to our own bodies, many of us neglect or take them for granted, just as I did. This is not a healthy or respectful relationship and I am on a mission to help you shift this.

## How improving the body-mind connection can help you

How many of us are at war with our bodies? We don't like how they look, or we get annoyed at the parts that don't function as we'd like them to. This creates disconnection, which counters to the 'integration' we're after. Some people go so far as to punish their bodies either by overeating or self-harming. Love and acceptance of our bodies, with all its strengths and shortcomings, is crucial for building a healthy partnership and setting one on the road to true potential. Body Talk can help heal the rifts we have with our bodies.

The link between your mind and body is not new – ancient and modern-day medicine recognize that many of our physical symptoms such as IBS and many stress related conditions including diabetes, heart disease and even cancer can have psychological or emotional roots.

People often come to see me because they can't sleep, they're having panic attacks due to stress, they may feel somehow removed from their daily life as if they were watching it through a glass; or they seem to have lost their enjoyment of life. I often see people become increasingly unhappy and disengaged from their lives – be that work, career, personal relationships or life – and yet their attempts at making things better seem to entrap them in behaviours that continue to punish their bodies. Imagine someone whose stressful job makes them ill but who just can't say no to a high-octane career, or someone who is in a toxic relationship but can't seem to leave. In all situations, it is the body that suffers.

Whilst we can't argue with sound advice such as maintaining a healthy diet, getting enough sleep and exercise, internally disconnected people will find it hard to implement these tactics because the four parts of their being – mind, heart, body and spirit – all want different things.

This is why I see Body Talk as a preventive and therapeutic method that can benefit anyone who wants to feel better and do better in life.

## Ambition demands physical fitness

Whilst ambition is a powerful driver and motivator, sustaining it demands physical wellbeing. Trying to push forward when you're internally disconnected is unwise and dangerous because the messages from our body to stop and rest are being ignored. Pushing through or working harder leads to abuse of the body through lack of sleep, and even substance abuse. In the face of pressure to get things done, much of the vital intelligence the body supplies goes unheard, leading to more stress, errors of judgment and bad decisions that waste time and effort. According to John Maule, Emeritus, Professor in Human Decision-Making and member of the Centre for Decision Research at the University of Leeds, when we're blocked from an important goal we experience stress.[7]

This stress occurs on many levels: for example, we may worry and be anxious, we may freeze or feel physically weakened through fear or experience a sense of helplessness. Worry tends to be distracting. It places a demand on our attention when in reality it is actually reducing our ability to think about effective action. Making decisions under stress makes it easier to overlook important information because the problem in hand becomes the focus. Stress also often leads to a false sense of urgency. We feel an urge to make fast decisions simply to remove the problem rather than find the wise solution. The need to solve a problem under duress tends to narrow our focus, leading to faulty thinking. Finally, stress makes it harder to control cravings, urges and can make us more susceptible to addiction. Basically, feeling under pressure forces our minds to work out of balance with our bodies and wisdom.

---

[7] Watch a helpful video interview with Prof John Mule for the Economist on how stress impacts decision-making http://decisionmaking.eiu.com/video/how-stress-impacts-decision-making/

I see integration being fundamental to 21st Century living. Today's lives present us with ever more stress. In his book *The Stress Solution*, Dr Rangan Chatterjee, a GP pioneer of holistic approach to medicine shows that over 85 per cent of adults experience daily micro stress doses on a regular basis.

Whether you're an athlete or stay- at-home parent, we all have plenty of demands on our mental, physical, emotional and spiritual stamina. The body is key in this.

## Our bodies and minds are intimately linked

I have coached clients who have disordered lives: frequent travellers with no sense of true home, professional nomads afraid to settle down, those afraid of being hurt by another person because they were hurt before and can't find a way to recover from their past.

The stress of fears we imagine as real can make us behave in ways that are counter to our happiness more often than we care to admit. Many of the people I work with want to feel good and be happy but feel stuck. For example, a person whose partner left them for another gets stuck reminiscing and idealizing about their past relationship, overindulging, making unhealthy choices and won't give dating a chance even though they deeply want to find someone that loves them and who they can love back.

I have seen and heard my clients' minds and hearts at war in constant tussles over judging their looks, giving explanations and reasons for why they can't take the next step; all the while their heart grieves and cries lonely tears. The one place where all of this is registered is, of course, the body. It is the body that will grow overweight on the overindulgence of wine and comfort meals; it is the body that will be vilified for looking unattractive. The vicious circle will simply continue because the mind, heart, body and spirit are disconnected.

Adversely, people who appear content and whose lives function well by living in balance enjoy better health. The longest longitudinal study of what it means to have a good life began in the 1930s and is still being carried out by Prof Robert Waldinger, a psychiatrist and Professor at Harvard Medical School. This unique study has been following 724 men (and later included women) to shed light on how psychosocial variables and biological processes from early childhood years links with their health and wellbeing in later life (in the 80s and 90s), what aspects of childhood and adult experiences correlate with the quality of intimate relationships one has in later life and how marriage is linked with health and wellbeing.[8]

A key insight Prof Waldinger and his team made, is that good relationships keep us healthy and happy far more than money and fame. The study confirms what we have always suspected about human beings being highly social. Social connections supplement our health while experience of loneliness literally kills us. According to Dr Waldinger, the study shows that "people who don't get as much connection as they need and want are less happy overall, their health declines

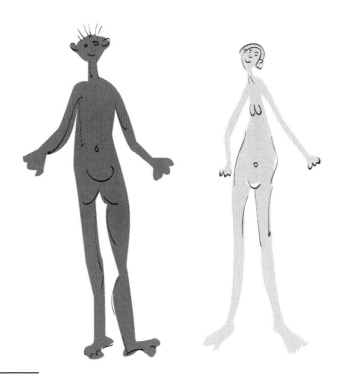

---

8   Find out more about the study here https://robertwaldinger.com/about-happiness/

earlier in midlife, their brain functioning declines sooner and they live shorter lives than people who are not lonely" [9].

People with a high degree of health seem to share the following characteristics: they report satisfaction in terms of self-realisation (happy mind), they cultivate meaningful connections with others (happy heart) and their lives have meaning (happy spirit). Based on what I see in my practice, I know that integration of mind, heart, body and spirit - in other words, the conscious attempt at balancing our physical, mental, emotional and spiritual needs - helps us stay healthier, live with more purpose and ultimately allows us to connect better with others and ourselves.

---

9   Access the study set up and relevant publications at: https://www.adultdevelopmentstudy.org/publications

## Our bodies know things our minds don't

Body Talk helps bring to conscious attention the deep knowledge that the mind may gloss over or even actively repress. Our bodies have a beautiful and profound wisdom at every level - from that of a single cell, to organs, systems, in fact our total makeup. Epigenetic research shows us that cells can store memories of experiences in the form of modified DNA and, even more surprisingly, we can pass these modifications on to our offspring.

Back in 2013, I was asked by my local Chapter of coaches what neuroscience could provide, by way of practical insights that they could apply in their practices. The question wasn't surprising. Being able to give clients facts and data plays to the natural dominance of the mind. Nowadays, coaches are keen to grasp how understanding the brain can help them become better at their job. Can it? Of course! My training and research work makes a massive difference in how I work with my clients and what can be achieved together because I can connect the theory with the practical know-how. Now let's look at some information that I think everyone could benefit from and be aware of.

Of all the papers I examined in the top neuroscience journals that year, one research study in the prestigious journal of Nature Neuroscience aroused my curiosity. It presented the work of Brian Dias and Kerry Ressler of Emory University who showed that mice can inherit fear across generations.

To study the phenomenon, Dias and Ressler trained mice to fear a specific smell by pairing it with an electric shock. Soon enough the animals learnt to associate the shock with the smell so that even when no shock was presented, the specific smell caused the mice to shudder in fear. The offspring of the mice also feared the same smell even though they never received the same training. Their pups (third generation) also feared the same smell. Could similar mechanisms be at play when it comes to depression, addiction, anxiety and many other conditions?

Often clients seek to understand why they keep making disempowering choices and here was research showing that bodies carried answers far better than minds. If those baby mice could talk, they would not be able to explain why they feared a specific smell. The behaviour would likely be irrational to them and yet very real. Sometimes when my own Body Talk practice brings something to my awareness, I find the same. I experience a feeling but struggle to explain it. Other times I find that I can't argue with the truth of it, but a part of me tries to deny it.

## Systems within systems in need of balance and integration

In 2017, I travelled to Scotland to train with Dr Lisa Schwarz, an American psychologist, therapist and pioneer of a technique called Comprehensive Resource Model (CMR). I was attracted to her work after reading a Newsweek article[10] describing her approach to healing trauma. Through demonstrations and tutorials, Lisa explained how clients could remember traumas and issues from gestation and even down their ancestry line. It deeply resonated with what I had seen in my own practice with clients and how, by integrating different methods, I was able to help them heal.

In trauma therapy, we work to recover the mind, heart, body and spirit from stressful events that have impacted the person deeply, making them less capable of facing and dealing with their present reality. Paying attention to the body here is critical. Simply put, the body remembers. It keeps account of how things feel and the impacts it experiences. Whilst the brain may not know how the body stores and uses that information, it can't help but be triggered by it. A trigger is simply something that surfaces an initial wounding memory, eliciting an immediate conditioned response that represents how we coped in adversity. For example, an adult who has been physically harmed as a child by an angry father may cower and go silent when someone raises their voice or adopts a facial expression that triggers their mind to imagine they are back in the angry parent scenario. The speed of such responses needs little cognition. They are automatic and habitual.

---

10      Matthew Green, "A Radical New Therapy Could Treat the 'Untreatable' Victims of Trauma," Newsweek, March 2017 https://www.newsweek.com/2017/03/31/trauma-ptsd-therapy-comprehensive-resource-model-treats-untreatable-572367.html

What our brain picks up from the body via different nerve fibres matters as much as what originates within it. If, for example, you feel sick in your stomach or tight from stress, your mind may recognise this as the time, long ago, when you experienced the fear of being beaten up at school, and this makes you anxious. The body feels and the mind interprets that feeling. This explanation may be wrong, but it may also be the best the mind has to offer or the most appropriate in terms of ensuring you're protected from potential danger. We can work with the mind but helping your body feel safe can be equally effective at giving your total-self a whole new experience so new learning can occur. In other words, it is not simply about teaching clients to think differently but also to feel differently, retraining the body to express itself from a healthy, unimpaired place.

The same applies with positive emotions that are often sought because they give us that good feeling. We want to belong, feel loved, be appreciated and respected. Every human being wants this. At the larger collective level, we harm each other through deliberate exclusion, judgment and withdrawal of love as much as by physical violence. Thus, we perpetuate traumas unless we stop long enough to pay attention to what's happening and on how our behaviour impacts others and ourselves. This can be done at different levels: inquiry and reflection, emotional connection and dialogue, direct physical observation and spiritual work that can be actioned on a daily basis.

Look around you. I bet you too will notice mind, heart, body and spirit at work within different communities you belong to: families, teams, organisations, countries and so on. And you will also no doubt notice when one or more of them are not engaged. In such moments, it is worth remembering that your presence matters more than you think! The key question is whether your mind, heart, body and spirit are alive and connected within you.

My Body Talk method tunes into the body and begins to learn to discern what is going on within it. This may include feeling various body parts for the state of our muscles - whether they are tight or relaxed - our heart rate, the pattern of our breathing, body alignment and posture, and energy flow. If this leaves you wondering if that's possible, let me assure you that it is. The more we pay attention to something with intention, the more discerning we become. And with it, we become more empowered and resilient.

THE BODY IS A MAJOR SUPERPOWER

# The Body is a Major Superpower

## Revealing your mind and body intelligences

If all this sounds rather abstract or improbable, try this quick exercise:

1. Close your eyes and bring to mind someone you cherish and love.

2. Bring your full attention to your body and notice how your body experiences this person. What do you feel inside? Pause here to connect with your body and this experience. You may feel a gentle warmth, a sense of spaciousness, relaxation, coziness, easing of internal muscle tension, calm, and so on.

3. Now, bring to mind a person or a situation that was mildly unpleasant and notice what effects this has on your body. Pause here to connect with your body and this experience. You may find that your body shivers and tightens. You may for example feel a physical block or constriction in your throat or chest; you may shrink away physically, make a facial gesture of unpleasantness, or feel tense. What is happening, in effect, is that your body is showing you how this person makes you feel. This demonstrates how our physical environments, and the people we surround ourselves with, impact us physically even if we try to deny it.

Over time, the body adapts to conditions whether they are ideal or less so. Our posture and stance, how we move and talk and what we think becomes a reflection of our regular experiences. The nervous system learns these patterns and behaviors and they quickly turn into habits.

By bringing non-judgmental curiosity to how your body is feeling in any given situation with Body Talk we can catch the physical place where we hold tension related to a specific memory, event or person.

We can work back through such memories and situations to help the body resolve these tensions and reset its response to what is true in the now and how we want things to be in the future.

For example, by working through how scary it was to go through a painful heartbreak and how scared we may still be when we are in conflict with someone we love, we can remember that the past and present differ and we can choose to respond differently. Body Talk gives you information that can help you become aware of the present and the past and with this the opportunity to consciously control how you respond in the moment.

The body constantly readjusts posture, muscle tension and energy through biofeedback received from the nervous system via the senses. This process is automatic, and mostly without our conscious awareness. With Body Talk you can train your attention so that you are more acutely aware when your body is trying to tell you something. In a busy world in which you rush about, such information can easily go amiss without a Body Talk practice. This means we're not only less aware of what's happening to us but also not fully engaged in the present moment. Because Body Talk reconnects you consciously with your body, the practice can help you feel more grounded and calm as well as alerting you to early signs of potential major issues before they get the chance to develop.

## Why modern life needs to practice Body Talk

Today's fast pace of life is putting more stress on the physical body. We sleep less, the quality of our food has worsened and many of the restorative practices such as being in nature, rest, and play have diminished. Quiet times of reflection or prayer, which are good for our wellbeing, have been traded for clearing the inbox and responding to constant bids for our attention.

For many people, the necessities of life such as keeping a job, paying rent and supporting loved ones or even our drive for self-actualisation makes paying attention to the state of the body harder simply because there is less time for it. Neurologically, being 'always on the go' is linked to high stress levels and illness such as heart disease, cancer and a battery of autoimmune diseases. As we're creatures of habit, and the nervous system is highly adaptable, our high-octane way of life becomes so habitual that we can't easily register the impact this is having on the body.

The more our minds stay engaged in thinking, the more difficult it can be to disconnect or stop thinking. Many clients I see struggle with a racing mind, overthinking and finding worries popping up as if they were in a video game. Regular interruptions are extremely tiring and disruptive to concentration, focus, and rest. The culture of always being informed and connected via technological devices makes switching off harder still. In my practice I see a trend of people prioritising results and work over everything else. Work trumps having a social or family life, life trumps looking after one's health until your health itself becomes a problem. What happens when we become ill? It is so ironic that we're fuelled by the desire to live longer, improve the quality of our lives and driven to experience more pleasure and yet, in the pursuit of a 'better' life, we encounter and create more suffering. The Dalai Lama puts his finger on it perfectly here:

BODY TALK

*"Man surprises me most about humanity. Because he sacrifices his health in order to make money. Then he sacrifices money to recuperate his health. And then he is so anxious about the future that he does not enjoy the present; the result being that he does not live in the present or the future; he lives as if he is never going to die, and then dies having never really lived."*
*Dalai Lama*

Whilst the body often comes last, we live and experience life through it. For me, the body is a sacred instrument for collecting and relaying

vital knowledge. When the mind disconnects from the body and functions at its expense, the body suffers. But with regular use of my easy-to-implement Body Talk practice, we can attend to the needs of our bodies along with our emotional and rational needs and help bring them into balance and harmony. We can help our bodies rebalance our minds and hearts by allowing our loving and compassionate selves to hear and interpret what our bodies are telling us. This way our physical body can become an equal partner in supporting our greatest aspirations. As we learn to work within our physical limits we are often able to transcend them.

## The capacity for connection and disconnection always exists

Numerous studies from childhood development, psychology of early attachment, positive psychology investigations into optimal cognitive performance, as well as PTSD and trauma work give us incredible insight into how and why we can become disconnected from our emotions, from our bodies or even from our spirit. Most of this work boils down to how our brains develop in the first place and the vital role that a felt sense of safety, connection to others, love and care play in helping us develop and maintain internal coherence. Without an early understanding of what feeling safe physically, mentally and emotionally actually feels like, the body has no safe place or basis for learning these states. Not knowing the baseline makes it harder if not impossible to aim for them later. As you will find elsewhere in this book, this can have marked negative consequences for the development of mental and emotional intelligence and for behavior itself.

The brain comes prepared to learn from experience. It converts experience into learning and memory. It works day and night to integrate and make sense of those woven narratives to create a consistent sense of who one is and what is one's subjective reality. If I am raised to believe the world is not safe, my natural orientation to the world will be anxiety in new situations. This mental state will be reflected in my physicality and how I relate to others. It is known as muscle memory. Just as my mind will remember where I should hide to avoid getting beaten, and I may remember the terrifying fear that went with it, my muscles will remember how to make me small enough to hide and therefore avoid getting hurt or how to escape the experience by disconnecting from it entirely.

# THE BODY IS A MAJOR SUPERPOWER

I remember meeting a young man who was abused by his carers as a schoolboy at a training course. For the first two days, he sat with his arms folded in a defensive position: his shoulders raised high with tension, lowered forehead and his eyes were constantly scanning everyone's faces and movements. He was in a state of high alert, as he did not feel safe. I got to know him well during our course and it was devastating to hear of the lasting impact his early years and trauma had on his ability to form healthy relationships, parent his kids and become a better human being. Imagine his mind working in overdrive constantly alert for possible dangers, the emotional disconnection from the fear of misjudging situations and people and the 'better be safe than sorry' approach he had learned which left him with a body that was unable to relax. Would you think this man's full spirit got to express itself and flow? No. This is why he came to the course.

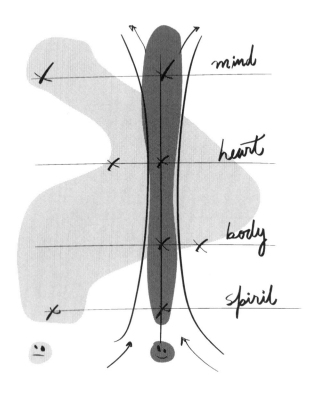

Traumatic events in later life have the power to once again kick the brain out of careful equilibrium and scramble our circuits, severely impacting the mind's perception of time, the meaning it attaches to specific stimuli and distortions in the storage and retrieval of memories. This happens because our brains remain open to experience, shape it and change in response to it.

## The brain pays attention to what happens within us

While the brain works as a whole, it's also subdivided into areas with specific functions. One area that is especially interesting when it comes to mind-body connection is called the insula. The brain naturally pays attention to itself and to the body. This process is known as interoception. The insula helps us feel the state of our body – hunger, satiety, sickness, temperature, and need for the toilet or sexual arousal. Interoception allows us to feel our emotions. This region of the brain has been shown to be involved in a number of functions such as self-awareness, perception and cognition. Our internal sense of how we are impacts our behaviour and how we feel. The insula also helps us sense how others are feeling.

The body and mind are wired and interconnected, readjusting and correcting in a way that will best deliver overall balance, also known as homeostasis. Discoveries in the last few years are revealing how all our major organs, our immune system and even our gut microbiota affect our brain function and that they, in turn, are affected by what happens in the nervous system.

The key message is this: honing our sense of interconnectedness gives us the best chance of developing awareness of what we need and what to focus on. So, if I start to become aware that nothing seems to touch me emotionally or that I am physically desensitised or over-sensitised to specific triggers, I now have the choice to address this. And this is why I believe mindful attention and becoming a conscious observer of what's actually going on in our bodies, how we are feeling and what thoughts are dominating our lives, can help us self-care and handle life's ups and downs with greater flexibility and resilience.

## Today's fast pace makes integration harder — unless we learn to pay attention

Our hyper-connected technological age is causing the very resource we need to be mindful - our attention - to become spent and is training it to disconnect us from ourselves. Our modern world is changing at a pace that is leaving many people scared and anxious. Admitting we are fearful can be even scarier but losing ourselves in a Netflix box set or a virtual reality game is both easy and tempting. We're generally prewired to do our best to escape reality when we don't feel safe. And we do this more often than we may realize. I invite you to contemplate for a moment how many of your recent decisions were motivated by fear versus love?

Increasingly, we are afraid to look vulnerable, show emotions, follow our dreams and connect deeply with what's happening within. Yet how can we understand and love others when we're struggling to self-know and self-accept ourselves? How are we to raise healthy well-adjusted children if we lack time and no longer value deep human-to-human connection or have few skills with which to do this?

Imagine yourself filled with a powerful mass of moving energy that you can direct to where you need it. Now imagine some of that energy being pooled or trapped in specific places making it inaccessible to you. Your connection to it has been cut - you're not operating on full power. This is what disconnection is like. It reduces both your resourcefulness and your effectiveness in life.

Let's take an analogy of the garden. You are a gardener tasked with tending a beautiful patch of greenery. If you make regular visits, monitoring how things are growing, regularly pruning and weeding, your garden will bloom. If you neglect your garden, the most dominant and established plants will survive and others may perish. Similarly, if you focus on just one patch, the remainder will grow wild and imbalanced. Your garden will not reach its full potential.

Integrating body, heart, mind and spirit follows the same principle. If we're not fully connected, our attention is directed to specific parts of us at the expense of our 'whole'. When I ask people in my workshops to consider what dominates their internal system, 95 to 98 per cent say it's their mind. Many comment that this is the way the world is rigged. This is to our detriment and we can do far better.

The mind needs rest. It refuels when we tap into the heart for love and compassion and when we sense reality not just through our mental filters but also equally with our greater embodied knowing. Having a felt experience to work from instead of an idea or thought about it grounds us in the only reality we need: the truth of what is.

When we become more integrated, the energy of our spirit flows and acts through us more readily. Being integrated helps us feel more alive, grounded and in control. In this state, fulfilment and vitality become easier. We can facilitate this work with Body Talk because the practice encourages us to slow down, connect with all parts of ourselves - body and feelings - and in the process use the mind resourcefully not as a slave driver, but as a caring custodian.

## Your internal system is in constant update mode

The body and nervous system are constructed so that much of the scanning and attention happens automatically – it's a subconscious activity. Different parts of the mind regularly attend to past memories and continuously reform them. Other parts monitor the state of the physical body, the impact of the world on it through the senses directing you towards what is more pleasant or aligned with what you want. However, when your attention becomes entangled in something for too long, it forgets everything else exists. This creates a natural imbalance.

## THE BODY IS A MAJOR SUPERPOWER

Have you ever experienced being so absorbed in something you were doing that when you finally detached from it, your body was stiff? Or a situation where you have been completely hijacked by an emotion, only to regret your actions later when your rational mind could appraise the situation from a calmer place and your body had returned to its natural equilibrium? Or what if you began to experience a longing for escape; travel or artistic creation because a part of your spirit was not being offered the opportunity to shine? These are perfect examples of how, within us, the mind, heart, body and spirit reminds us of their presence and needs. All we must do is pause, attune to their messages, listen and integrate that into the totality of our experience.

The body constantly monitors and senses what is happening around and within us through biofeedback mechanisms. If we want to achieve greater integration of mind and body, we need to recognise and attend to this process.

To experience the physical body, we need to register it with our minds and our emotions. Usually we do the opposite, telling the body how it 'should' feel or how it 'should' behave.

Have you ever consciously experienced yourself walking? What it feels like as your weight shifts from one leg to the other? Or, how you physically feel whilst walking on a busy pavement or on an empty train. When you think about it, each of these experiences is deeply felt. They elicit specific feelings in the body. As we begin to pay attention to them, they provide us with vital information and the opportunity to adjust our thoughts, emotions and our physicality. Rather than be at the mercy of something happening in the background, we can discover and choose what is best for us with authority.

It's simple – within us we have all the tools necessary to help. Our mind can be our biggest ally when we learn to manage it well.

## Awareness builds with practice

Often, the first time my clients experience many of the body feeling states is when we do 'embodied' activities together. "I got hurt" is no longer a thought. It is a realisation that is visceral, emotional and cognitive. Through integrative activities, their range of detection and awareness increases, and imbalances shift. They discover more choices and a more finely tuned instrument of detection.

For example, Anna is a marketing executive who comes to see me because she struggles with confidence making pitches to clients. Anna battles with her mind. Whilst part of her criticises how she performs, another part is constantly watching out, her inner critic trying to deflect critical thoughts about her performance. Pitches, therefore, are stressful and draining. Anna's mind has learned to be distracted from the sense of discomfort in her body, which manifests as tightness of the chest and stomach, a high-pitched voice and red rash. Anna is not numb to what's happening to her body. She is deeply anxious of it doing things she can't control. At the same time as her frequent disconnection at work, Anna has also identified a sense of "not being fully present " when spending time with her partner and children.

Working together, she learned to gently change her experience of pitching by changing what she pays attention to.  By teasing apart what is causing each symptom, Anna's mind and body has worked out a new reality, one in which the people in the room are also fellow mothers and fathers, instead of strangers with important jobs and little time that Anna needs to impress. As Anna has practiced these new strategies she has become conscious of feeling grounded in her feet as she stands to make her PowerPoint presentations, she also begins to recognise how much they actually support her. This makes her feel calmer. Through connecting with her body, Anna is able to find a new sensation to pay attention to: the feeling of strength from standing with authority at the front of the room. This has had a massive transformation on Anna's work performance to the extent where she began to enjoy presenting to clients. The change was also far reaching. Anna returned one day and advised me she was "less often in her head" and worried less about many other things that used to keep her awake at night.

The reason why connecting mind, heart, spirit and body works is that our nervous systems only believe what it concludes from experience. So when the body dominates an experience by being super-stressed and nervous, that is the overriding result. For example, you may be speaking in front of a group and you become aware of your heart pounding loud and your face flushing red. As you become aware of these body sensations, your mind concludes that you're incredibly nervous and you feel nervous, anxious and more stressed. Similarly, calmness also results from a specific mixture of thoughts, feelings and sensations. If you're breathing slowly and deeply your mind notices that those deep breaths indicate you're not in danger. The more your body relaxes, the more pleasant you feel and your mind begins to believe you're calm. You could in fact be feeling calm doing this whilst facing a Rottweiler simply because you believe that by staying genuinely calm you won't trigger the dog to attack you.

As we pay more attention to the body we can detect this miraculous process of thoughts, feelings, sensations and perceptions intermixing as a constant stream of information. By choosing where we place our attention, we can adjust our experience to our advantage, instead of being habitually hijacked and out of balance.

Because bodies have no reasons to mask what's true, with Body Talk, we connect to the physical body to find out how things are. With practice, we learn to notice and gauge how we can change things for the better. As the mind sees and hears the body report on its feelings and truths, it learns that our experience can change. We can become healthier, calmer, more grounded and joyful. The evidence for this is real and felt in our bodies. Body Talk helps us operate from how things are instead of how we want them to be so that even if what we're feeling or thinking is not ideal, our best chances of transforming and transcending our circumstances come from facing and working with what is.

## The body is our superpower

We are at our most powerful when we are fully present and in our bodies. Life happens in the present moment – we can't exist in the past or the future – and the degree to which we experience life 'in the now' gives us our 'aliveness' – a quality which shines through to others. Prejudices, hatred, a closed heart and dissociation can however make us numb to the 'now' within and to each other.

Our key defense and tool for being superhuman is being fully human.

## Burnout happens because we stop paying conscious attention

Neglecting or abusing our bodies creates stress. Chronic stress has been linked to a number of the most pressing modern health conditions such as diabetes, heart attacks and cancer. Stress is also associated with most inflammatory diseases such as lupus, IBS, and chronic fatigue syndrome. Even if our genes predispose us towards one or another form of illness, the weight of clinical and non-clinical studies into self-care shows us that how we look after ourselves, how we balance our mental, emotional, physical and spiritual needs, affects our genes, our moods, our health and healing.

As shown by Dr Waldinger's Good Life study, making conscious choices to have loving and supporting communities of friends and partners as well as loving ourselves enough to choose well are vital for our ability to live well. Often, the reality of this is the seemingly small choices we make on a regular basis. Do we choose to stay mindful of the present? Do we remember to acknowledge what is good in our life and its many blessings? Do we consider whether what we eat serves us well? Does how we spend our time really serve us? At a time when paying attention seems harder than ever, not paying attention is the worst choice of all.

Burnout is one far too frequent outcome of not paying attention to the balance between the needs of our mind, heart, body and spirit. The world is in a burnout crisis. In the search for what we believe should matter, we're in danger of losing what matters to us! A study conducted by Gallup in 2017 found that two-thirds of all full-time workers experienced burnout. An American psychologist Herbert Freudenberger first coined burnout as a term in the 1960s. Freudenberger noticed a phenomenon whereby a person with burnout was so exhausted that they had difficulty coping with life and their current demands. Originally the term was used in relation to the "helping" professions such as doctors and nurses. However, with 24/7 working, access to unprecedented levels of technology and the many fears of the modern workplace, including redundancy as well as the rise of artificial intelligence, incidents of burnout are increasing.

I have witnessed this first hand as a coach and personal counselor to many individuals. Many people struggle to remain unaffected by the physical, mental and emotional demands everyday life places on them. This is an alarming trend given greater awareness and well-intentioned interventions by government, employers and organisations.

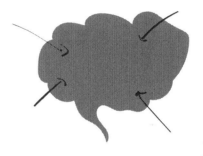

An article in the 2017 April issue of Harvard Business Review[11] quoted massive healthcare spending costs connected with burnout. It estimated cost was somewhere between $125 and $190 billion per year. What is less clear is how we translate these numbers in terms of the individuals' sense of confidence to remain resilient in the future? Or the burden that one person's burnout places on others, across work and family systems?

What is far more alarming is that a 2017 study in PLOS One,[12] one of the most highly ranked academic journals, linked job burnout with health risks such as diabetes, coronary heart disease, high cholesterol and even death. It seems that all these pressures drive people's minds, bodies and hearts to fail.

As the historian and philosopher Yuval Noah Harari writes in his latest wise book *21 Lessons for 21st Century* , in a world where we expect to live longer and have more access to information than ever before, it is change itself that may exhaust us. According to him, what we need most is mental flexibility and emotional balance.

The body is a physical outlet for the mind, our emotions (what I refer to as the heart) and for the state of our spirit. I have seen many cases and indeed experienced in my own life, how the body tries to claim back the energy it has 'lent' to the mind or the heart in pushing to get things done or processing emotions. The constant 'borrowing' against the body's energy creates anxiety, stress and eventually disease. I have seen in my coaching and therapeutic practice how emotional needs for love and connection can morph into soothing pangs of

---

11  Eric Garton, "Employee Burnout Is a Problem with the Company, Not the Person" Harvard Business Review, April 06, 2017.
12      Salvagioni DAJ, Melanda FN, Mesas AE, Gonzalez AD, Gabani FL, Andrade SMD. (2017) Physical, psychological and occupational consequences of job burnout: A systematic review of prospective studies. *PLOS ONE* 12(10): e0185781.

hunger that won't satiate no matter how much food is consumed and how not paying attention to what's happening can make clients gain weight that makes them loathe themselves. It's a vicious cycle.

I have watched clients seek new thrills and experiences in order to avoid feeling vulnerable in their relationships, foolishly thinking that their partner will somehow fill their own voids. And I have been in these places myself, making the same errors and learning how each mistake happened because my mind, heart, body and spirit were in constant conflict. When we omit to pay our body attention and work to a state of exhaustion, we risk burnout: a complete mental, emotional and physical overwhelm. This condition is disempowering, but it also gives us a necessary cue that we've veered off a sensible path. It is largely avoidable and I am passionate about equipping people with the tools to stop this happening.

Body Talk isn't designed to replace your doctor or any medical interventions. You need their professional expert opinions when you are unwell. But Body Talking can help you avoid burnout by giving you the information you need to adjust your lifestyle so that your body is not pushed past its limits. It will give you a massive arsenal of observations that will help your doctor understand better what may be going on when you're unwell and aid a correct diagnosis.

## A final word before we Body Talk...

What attracted me to neuroscience was a fascination with how 'plastic' the brain is. I always marveled at its capacity for growth and change. Many of the best coaching sessions I have had with clients have come not from knowing what is and is not possible, but from trusting our mutual experiences and being curious. We find the answers together. In other words, bringing our minds, hearts, bodies and spirits to the work makes all the difference.

I came to learn that the same is true of the body. Ask any yoga teacher or rehabilitation expert and they will tell you that with practice, the body becomes stronger, more flexible and able to do more. The process, however, requires our full presence: mind, heart, body and spirit. So, let's start to reconnect with the body now, to strengthen our health and performance to achieve our most optimal health and performance.

# Let's talk:
# 5 Activities to Kickstart a Conversation with Your Body

*"Our body is precious.
It is our vehicle for awakening.
Treat it with care."*
Buddha

## LET'S TALK: 5 ACTIVITIES TO KICKSTART A CONVERSATION WITH YOUR BODY

In this section you will find five of my favorite exercises devised to begin a dialogue with your body. The five activities are designed to follow one another and help you:

1. Understand and connect with your felt sense (Exercise 1).

2. Begin a conversation with your body (Exercise 2).

3. Discover how you can capture body parts' own stories and truths by tuning into your body and creating a body-map (Exercise 3).

4. Develop your relationship with your body through repeated dialogue (Exercise 4).

5. Gain awareness into the relationship you have with your body (Exercise 5).

I recommend you attempt all these activities in sequence. However, you may find that one or two really resonate with you and you can start there also. If you experience a strong feeling of resistance to a particular activity, note it. Paradoxically, this is another cue that the exercise may be the best one to tackle. If you're a practitioner, initially invite your clients to experience all activities in the sequence provided and assist them if required. Once your client is familiar with the work, you can pick and choose those that best fit their needs.

Many of my clients who complete these activities with me often go, "Wow!"

They discover just how dominant their mind can be and begin to appreciate that there is more to them than their rational ego voice. At other times, they will say "But I already knew this!" To this I smile and reply, "Precisely!" Now you are in a different state of knowing.

Let me give you an analogy.

Imagine being vaguely aware that your son or daughter is seeking your attention but you are brushing them off and not giving him or her your full loving concern. Then imagine your child in the future, marching up to you and saying, "Dad/Mum, there are times when you brushed me off as if I did not matter to you and that hurt!"

Notice how much more powerful this second awareness is when you have no choice but to hear your child's truth.

This is what Body Talk can do for you – it can give you conscious intentional awareness of a crucial part of you that you may be brushing off.

LET'S TALK: 5 ACTIVITIES TO KICKSTART A CONVERSATION WITH YOUR BODY

## EXERCISE 1: FELT SENSE

**Time:** 10-15 minutes

**You will need:** a quiet space, a pen, and your journal (if you wish to make notes).

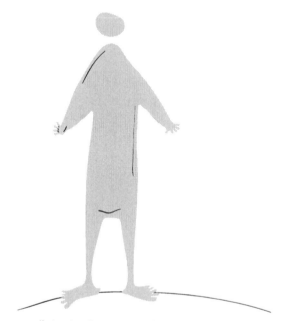

*"The body is a multilingual being.
It speaks through its color and its temperature, the flush of recognition,
the glow of love, the ash of pain, the heat of arousal,
the coldness of non-conviction...
It speaks through the leaping of the heart, the falling of the spirits,
the pit at the center and rising hope"*
Clarissa Pinkola Estés, American poet, Jungian psychoanalyst, post-trauma recovery specialist

Our bodies express our true spirit and essence. They reflect what we think and feel - our deepest truths - because they store all our experiences within. We can access this knowledge through a deeply intuitive felt sense.

This exercise helps you discover this bodily (somatic) and deeply integrative experience that transcends thoughts, feelings, and sensations. To experience it for yourself in a conscious and mindful way, I invite you to place yourself in three specific scenarios. Simply observe how it feels to be in them.

## Felt Sense exercise instructions

Find a comfortable position and establish a mindful attention with how your body feels. Tune into your head, neck, shoulders, arms, torso, stomach, pelvis, hips, legs and feet. Begin to get a general awareness of any sensations that are present in your body. You may also notice the feeling of the clothes you're wearing, the weight of your hands resting on your lap for example, or your posture and muscle tension. You may get a sense of warmth or feel cold. Simply breathe and stay present.

Read each scenario below. Pause after each one and notice the overall felt sense you experience as you imagine yourself in each situation.

## Scenario 1

Imagine it's a cold and rainy day and you are feeling mildly chilly. Someone you know, trust and love offers you the soft, cozy and warm blanket and gently wraps it over your shoulders so that you nestle into it. Notice the response in your body as you imagine this scene. Notice if your breathing has changed. What about your heartbeat? Have your muscles relaxed or tensed? Consider the feelings you are experiencing in your body and describe the felt sense as you imagine yourself warming, feeling safe and attended to.

## Scenario 2

Imagine driving a car along a freeway when suddenly a car comes racing towards you against traffic. You are caught off guard and you realize that you will most likely have a head-on collision. How does your body respond?

## Scenario 3

Imagine seeing a young puppy or another animal's eyes meeting your eyes. You find their gaze kind, innocent, loving and deeply connecting. Allow yourself to really register the feeling of being seen and seeing this young creature relating to you in such an inviting and loving way. Notice how your body responds.

## Working with what you feel

1. Compare the felt experience in all three examples. How similar are they? What is different in terms of how they affect you? Notice the range of visceral reactions, emotions and thoughts that are possible from each one.

2. Now imagine the next project, goal or task you must do. You may also experiment with recalling a specific person in your life that you want to consider. Notice your felt sense in relation to it or to them. How does your body react? What do you observe happening in your body?

3. Complete the questions that follow.

## Reflective questions:

1. How would your cosy blanket response change if you were, for example, in a state of total shock? Or if the surface of the blanket irritated your skin? Or if you felt angry at the person who brought it to you?

2. How would your felt sense change for scenario 2, if you were a professional car racer or if you knew the scenario was a virtual reality game?

3. How would being seen with kind, loving eyes (scenario 3) change if you were incredibly late for an appointment you felt you could not miss or if there was a crying baby in the background?

4. How does what you think and believe impact on what you sense in relation to the chosen project, goal, task or person?

5. What conclusions can you draw from this?

Most people will discover that without having to think much about the situations, each scenario creates a certain physiological response that will vary from person to person depending on their previous experience and current state. In other words, without having to think much about what we think or feel, our bodies can't help but experience situations and surroundings. They do this constantly without us needing to pay attention.

Such felt sense gives us vital clues to our starting point from which we perceive, feel and act. It will determine what we can and can't do in a specific situation. Different choices become possible in our responses as we feel relaxed and at ease as opposed to when we feel anxious or threatened. By checking in with our felt sense, we become conscious of what is true and more able to use our mind to adjust our thinking and behaviour.

## EXERCISE 2: BODY BROADCAST

**Time:** 20 minutes

**You will need:** a pen and a quiet space. Write your answers below or in your journal.

*"My body gives me a regular readout
of how well I am doing in the world.
All I have to do is pay attention and listen.
Together, we do better!"*
Magdalena Bak-Maier, Neuroscientist, integration pioneer, and healer

# LET'S TALK: 5 ACTIVITIES TO KICKSTART A CONVERSATION WITH YOUR BODY

Your body is home to the most powerful force: You! Look after it, listen to it.

In this exercise, you're going to imagine that your body is telling the story of what it's like to live with you. It will speak into a microphone whilst you listen.

Start by adopting a comfortable siting position and set your intention to simply be present and open to what your body may tell you. Tune into your body by relaxing into it, as if you were sitting there with an old friend who is on your side but who just needs to tell you a few home truths. Know that they wish the best for you and that you have nothing to fear but much to gain from their insights.

From this place, give your body permission to complete the statements below. Trust that your body knows. Allow the answers to naturally emerge from within you and not from your mind or your ego. It will feel as though what is speaking is a deeper knowing. You may wish to write the answers in a journal or make a recording.

1. Hello. I belong to _____

2. Here's what it's like to be me on a typical day with you _____

3. The best I ever felt was in _____. I was _____

4. What I am here for is _____

5. When I'm not well, I _____

6. What I need most is _____

7. I feel deeply loved when _____

8. I feel disrespected when _____

9. I feel punished when _____

10. The stance I adopt most often is _____. And the impact of this on you is _____

11. The way I move when I'm at ease is _____

12. When I feel anxious or stressed, I _____

13. Most often I am _____

14. You can help me most by _____

15. The wisdom I would like to teach you right now is _____

Complete this activity by saying this affirmation to yourself:

*"I belong to you my body and you belong to me.
We are one!"*

When you have finished, read what your body told you. You will know that your body spoke to you when you sensed your mind almost going off to one side, listening and witnessing what was being said and knowing that it was not your mind speaking.

## LET'S TALK: 5 ACTIVITIES TO KICKSTART A CONVERSATION WITH YOUR BODY

Often in doing this exercise, people discover that initially the first set of answers will come entirely from their mind. Be alert to a tiny shift of awareness that may arise in you when this happens. It is your body gently, emotively letting you know, it is not me who's speaking here. If this happens, thank your mind for stepping in and reassure it that you value it. Then repeat the exercise, this time reflecting the truth from the body's point of view.

Go back to your written transcript or notes to highlight the essential information.

Notice what your body needs to best support you. For example, your body may tell you that it feels put upon and tired. How can you attend to it and use your mind's intelligence to do something productive about that and maybe treat it to some relaxation and rest. You may realize that what surfaced in dialogue with your body are deeper worries and needs such as what you really want but may not be getting from your partner or another person close to you. This awareness will give you vital clues about what to ask of them. You may actually notice that your body is your true friend in spite of how it functions or malfunctions for you. This is especially helpful for people who blame their body when it is unable to keep pace with their aspirations.

Often a genuine dialogue such as this will help you face and see your true body (gorgeous, toned, flabby, aging) and not the one you are deceiving yourself with. For example, as a diabetic, I often feel tired when my sugar level is too high. Detection of any muscle ache or lethargy makes my mind race with concern about my blood sugar reading, making me worried sick about the progress of my disease. But this often leads to counter-productive behaviour. Instead of motivating me to go outside for a run to strengthen my muscles, it can quickly make me feel so sorry for myself and I can become physically unable to move in a way that is literally crippling.

Having spoken to other diabetics who also need to measure their blood sugar on a regular basis, I can see for myself why, at times, it's so hard to prick your finger and again experience that awful sinking feeling. When I Body Talk in such moments, I may become aware of my legs saying "We want to contribute. Let's go for a walk now! We feel strong!" and by listening to them and hearing their message arising in my awareness, my mind can't ignore the fact that a part of me feels strong and completely capable. This experience shifts the outcome and I am off for the jog or run that I need to be well.

Doing this exercise may help you remember and reignite a sense of lightness and ease from a time when you had fun doing something you truly love or how you felt as a happy, carefree child. It will give you vital clues about how to return to your true purpose of living a fulfilling life. Whatever you find, allow that intelligence to guide you one little step towards feeling and being better.

## Reflection Points

Use the space below to answer these questions.

1. Describe the relationship you have with your body at this moment in time.

2. Does the way you presently relate with your physical self serve you both well?

3. How does your present relationship with your body need adjusting to achieve greater harmony and parity?

4. Given your answers above, imagine that you are giving a live radio broadcast. Would you feel good telling the world how you treat your body at the moment?

5. Is there anyone in your life, now or in the past, that you may have or are treating in a similar way to how you presently treat your physical body? For example, if you neglect a part of your body, do you also neglect your current partner and their needs? Often the way we relate with our bodies and what is going on in our lives mirror each other. Changing how we relate to ourselves often transforms how we are with others and vice versa.

# EXERCISE 3 : BODY MAP

**Time:** 10 minutes

**You will need:** a pen and your journal.

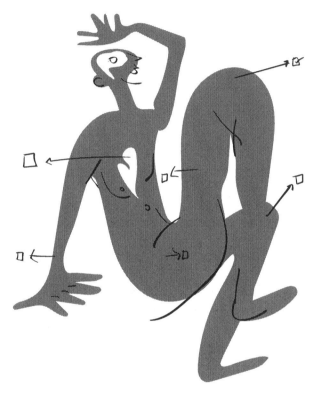

*"As long as you keep secrets and suppress information,
you are fundamentally at war with yourself.
The critical issue is allowing yourself to know what you know.
That takes an enormous amount of courage."*
Bessel A. van der Kolk,
Clinician, leading researcher and teacher in the area of post-traumatic stress

## LET'S TALK: 5 ACTIVITIES TO KICKSTART A CONVERSATION WITH YOUR BODY

Our bodies carry all our experiences within them. When they are not allowed to speak or when we fail to listen to them, key information about our true feelings, pressures, potential conflicts, experiences or issues we need to surface and address become buried. As Bessel A. Van Der Kolk says in the quote and in his powerful book The Body Keeps the Score, what we want from our body is to create a peaceful and fruitful relationship with our mind. We no longer want the body to keep secrets. We want it to tell us what's happening or what happened in the past so we have the opportunity to heal and do better for ourselves in the present and future.

In this exercise, we learn to tune into our body by drawing it on paper. We tap into the flow of a quick sketch in order to bypass the mind and access the deeper, less conscious element of intuitive knowing. What we hope to capture in the sketch is a sense and feel of the body rather than its exact form. Therefore, your drawing skills are not relevant to this activity. I encourage you to waste zero time thinking about whether you're doing this right - simply give it a go. This activity also forms a key element of the Body Talk practice, so I invite you to give it a try here.

After making a representational drawing that feels right, you are invited to begin a conversation with specific parts of your body to develop your listening skills.

1. Using your journal or a piece of paper, draw a quick outline of your body. Do it as quickly as possible by following your intuition. Avoid over-thinking it or agonising over detail - you are not aiming to produce a work of art or an exact likeness of yourself. Simply imagine your shape pouring out onto the page directly from your hand. You may end up standing, sitting, being small or big, facing forward, back or in profile. Trust that your hand will know what to do.

2. Once you have your drawing, put a 'x' in places where your body presently feels pain or discomfort. Aim for no more than three areas. If you are pain-free, mark the places that you're most aware of in your body in terms of having palpable energy.

3. After you've marked your drawing, go back to each mark in turn and spend a moment connecting with that particular place on or in your physical body. For each place, ask your body, not your mind, "What is the truth of this place/part?"

You may want to close your eyes as you do this. Imagine you're simply showing up ready to listen. Tune into what may well feel like nothing more than an intuitive knowing, faint suspicion or simply the truth. Note that the answer may or may not come as a phrase. It may be an image, a colour or something else. It may be an observation, a request or a comment. Bodies don't talk the same way minds do but the answer tends to arise from the body instead of the mind. So, allow the answer to bubble up from within you. Trust that your body knows how to answer this question even if your mind defensively protests or questions "How do I do this?" or wants to give up saying "I don't know how to do this!"

This way of listening to your deeper intelligence will help you connect more deeply with what is true for your body. You may also hear nothing but silence: that is a sign that your body is not ready to reveal its truth just yet. Should this happen, simply persist in your practice. Sometimes you may get silence for a long time. Imagine you're working with something that may have been hurt, wounded or unsure whether you will listen. Patience, gentleness and openness to keep practicing is key here. That said, most clients can always pinpoint at least one area that is giving them trouble and establish a communication with it fairly quickly.

4. Answers may take time to develop but that is why Body Talk is a process and method for deepening your mind-body dialogue and mind, heart, body, spirit integration. So, for example, a first answer for lower back pain may be "too much work and too little play". Subsequent conversations however may reveal further details such as "fear of being poor", "lack of trust towards partner", "mild depression" and so on. The truth of what arises will find its resonance in your heart, mind and spirit. Whatever your body says, welcome its truth simply as information you can act on. If it feels right, you will sense it. Good or bad, you can then tap into the true power of your mind as a problem solver to either adjust what you're doing or maintain what works. My invitation to you in this exercise is to practice deep listening without judgment or defensiveness as your body speaks to you.

You might like to finish this exercise with the Loving Kindness Body Meditation which you will find on pg 120.

# EXERCISE 4: 7-DAY BODY DIALOGUE

**Time:** 5 minutes for 7 days (they don't have to be consecutive)

**You will need:** a pen, a quiet space and your journal to record your answers.

*"Health is the result of
all attempts to use the body lovelessly."*
A Course in Miracles *by* Marianne Williamson, American author,
spiritual leader, politician, and activist

LET'S TALK: 5 ACTIVITIES TO KICKSTART A CONVERSATION WITH YOUR BODY
---

By now, you are aware that your body has a voice and it wants to tell you what it needs. Your challenge is to tune into what it is saying.

In this exercise, you are invited to amplify the voice of your body so that you can learn what it needs from you and build your confidence. Like any good friendship, the more often you take the time to listen, the more you will hear.

Over the course of seven days you are invited to connect with your body over one simple question:

*"What do you need, body?"*

You can do this 5-minute exercise anywhere. If possible close your eyes for a moment to allow yourself to go inward with your attention. Connect with your breathing; notice your breath as it passes in and out of your body. Simply enjoy being present. Now, ask yourself "What do you need body?"

Make a note of the first answer that rises up in your awareness. Write it down below or in your journal.

You may notice that your mind jumps in offering an answer, but stay with the practice and simply breathe and be patient. Relax into the experience and the asking. The trick is not to try too hard, instead trust your body to speak for and to you.

For example, your mind may say, "I need to eat healthily" but what may arise from your body is "I need intimacy". Or, your body may say "I want to kick back and walk the green fields" but your mind is cramming work to get you ahead in your work.

Again, when you receive an answer, write it down.

This is a great way to find out about your body's true needs. But what if you're in the midst of a crunch or stressful situation? In such cases, you may want to ask your body what it needs right now from you. This is really helpful as a way to realign your mind and body and bring them into better balance at a time when disconnection is most likely. Remember how in such crunches most, or all your attention will often be focused on the problem your mind is contemplating. This can cause tension and stress that will accumulate in your body. It need not be this way. Your body can, in such situations, be turned into a valuable resource - by simply asking it about your immediate needs, wisdom and advice.

When I face stressful times I often enquire: "Dear body, what do you need or wish for me in this difficult situation?" An answer will often arise as if it were brought up from the depths of the ocean: "take a ten minute walk in the park and just breathe" – and I know this is both wise and good advice.

After seven days, look back and notice what your body has said or asked you for. Think about how you might respond. Commit to actioning specific request(s) so that you and your body create a supportive and loving partnership instead of being at war with each other.

Below I've given you a simple framework for recording your answers and action plans over seven days. There's a space to tick off the actions as completed and also to reflect on how the action felt when you were doing it. We will make use of this practice during the Body Talk process.

LET'S TALK: 5 ACTIVITIES TO KICKSTART A CONVERSATION WITH YOUR BODY

| Day | Message received from the body | Follow up action or simple acknowledgement (e.g. "I hear you!") | Action is completed |
|---|---|---|---|
| | I need hugs from my family | I need to ask my partner and child for this and explain to them how lovely it feels when they hug me. | ◊ done Jan 19th 2019 |
| | I need a massage | Schedule this for next week | ◊ done Feb 3, 2019 |
| | | | ◊ |
| | | | ◊ |
| | | | ◊ |
| | | | ◊ |
| | | | ◊ |
| | | | |
| | | | |

This simple exercise invites you to notice your body as a living, breathing being with its own needs. Much like those of a small child, these needs can only be met when your mind attunes to your body's gentle whisper and allows space for its messages to surface. When your body's needs are identified, named and met, your mind and body will find greater harmony and balance. This is fundamental for health and wellbeing and the good news is, it's entirely within your gift.

LET'S TALK: 5 ACTIVITIES TO KICKSTART A CONVERSATION WITH YOUR BODY

## EXERCISE 5: BODY TIMELINE

**Time:** 20 minutes

**You will need:** a quiet space, pen and paper or your journal to record your answers. You have the option to draw a timeline of your life or to walk along an imaginary timeline. If you're walking, you'll need some floor space.

*"I am always in relationship with my physical body.
The relationship I have with it profoundly influences my life
and I can change my life
by working on this relationship."*
Magdalena Bak-Maier, Neuroscientist, integration pioneer, and healerr

Imagine being a small baby. For the most part, babies don't really think about their physical form. At some point however, children become aware of their body; how it is presented, dressed and what it looks like. As we grow, we form an intimate relationship with our body that continues to evolve as we age.

Our sense of whether our body feels well or not starts early on. All along, our nervous system has been literally growing up with us. When you hear an infant cry because their nappy is soaked or they are too hot or cold, they already have a sense of what's comfortable and good and what is less so. We see this miracle in action when a small child says, "Mummy, my throat feels funny". Then one day that same child comes home telling you that they wish they were less tall or maybe slimmer than they are. Perhaps your own relationship with your body needs work. You may feel your body is betraying you, aging, getting sick when what you need is cooperation.

All along, the mind has been learning about what feels good, comfortable, "normal" or "average" to create a baseline. Over time, this baseline has been modified through habits, patterns, and circumstances, often just beyond our full attention. When this experience changes, the mind registers change and this may trigger attention. Such attention, in my view, ought to be paid to our bodies throughout our lives. However, as you will be aware, often the only time we focus on our body is when we are unwell. This is too late.

In this exercise, we will examine the relationship you presently have with your body. We will then go back and forward in time to establish how your body felt and how you would like it to feel. As we do this, we will also be able to clarify the sort of relationship you presently have, have had and may wish to have with your body going forwards. This will help shift habitual ways of being into conscious and healthier relations between your mind and body.

Finally, while you may want to do this activity using a piece of paper, you can also do this exercise moving around on an imaginary timeline on the floor.

Let's go!

**Exercise**

Step 1: The Now

Take a seat and connect with your physical body. To do so, take a few relaxing and centering breaths. You may want to close your eyes and relax your brow.

The goal is to tune into your body and simply be present with it. Notice how it feels.

What is the dominant sense within it? For example stress, tension, sadness, joy, aches, sexual desire, coziness, vitality, etc.

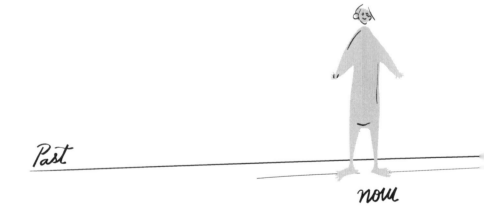

If you're doing this activity standing up, you may want to choose an object to represent you. Place this object somewhere in the room and stand to one side of it. This will allow you to report on yourself from a third position. This slightly detached perspective can be very helpful for some people. If the felt sense and emotions that you suspect will arise may be upsetting, such distancing will help protect you from feeling them directly. If you use an object you will be commenting on it as you.

I often use this method when conducting this activity with my clients in person. After choosing an object to represent them or standing in their present self, I invite them to tell me what is true here. I then ask them to imagine a timeline and show me where past and future are. Then, either standing to one side or walking the line, the client and I can work with time as explained below.

The two questions to answer in the present are:

1. How is my body feeling right now?

2. If you had to describe the relationship you have with your body at this moment in time what would it be? For example, the body

could be a best friend or an obstacle. The relationship could be ambivalent.

Whatever you discover here is very useful because you are deliberately noticing what is true.

Step 2: Looking back in time

If you're following this activity on paper, draw your timeline as illustrated above. You may want to separate this line into specific segments that will make sense to you. For example, you may want to subdivide the line into decades, specific life periods such as school or jobs you've held. Find a way that feels right and works for you. One client I worked with separated her line into two parts: before her partner died and after. The segments you make will match your life, your reality and what you need from this activity.

If doing this exercise standing up, imagine your life-line extending from your current position towards the moment of your birth in the given direction that feels right to you. For some people, the line may extend to their left, or behind them, but I encourage you to experiment until you notice a feeling in your body that tells you "This is it for me!"

Now walk along this line, or to the side of it if you're moving an object to represent you, making stops along the way in places that correspond to key segments with particular meaning for you.

Wherever you choose to stop, answer these two questions:

1. What was the dominant experience at this point for my physical body?

2. How would I describe my relationship with my body at this time point?

When you complete all the time point segments you want to explore, make a note about what your body and you have been through. Note how your mind and body related to one another.

Also, notice how the way you relate to your body has evolved over the years towards what is now.

You and your body certainly have an incredible history. You have been through a great deal. And like the best of friendships, it is worth taking a moment to pause and consider what you want and need from each other for the future.

Step 3: Looking forward

It's now time for you to look ahead to make a conscious choice about how you want your body to feel – how you want to relate to it. Whether you're doing this on paper or standing up, look ahead literally as if you're looking forward in time or if you're happy to step forward, move along the line towards the future and allow your body to experience how it feels doing that.

Take a moment to center yourself and breathe four to six loving deep breaths, inhaling the qualities you want to retain (for example resilience, strength, vitality) and exhaling those you want to purge (for example fatigue, weakness, frailty).

As with looking back in time, you may want to separate this timeline into specific periods. For example, I often ask clients to consider how they want to feel in three to six months, a year from today and in three years.

If you're doing this activity standing, return to the present moment and imagine the line extending towards your future self. Some people feel their future may go straight ahead or to the right of them whilst their past may extend behind or to their left. Each person is different. Follow your intuitive sense.

As you move forward along your timeline, consider these two questions.

3. How do you want your body to feel at specific time points? For example, you may wish to stop along your future line six months, a year or three years from now. It is useful to attune to the specific time point instead of just a general future. At each place, tune into your body and see if you can pick up a felt sense of what your body wants to experience.

4. What sort of mind-body relationship will best support this? What do you need to do differently to ensure this is achieved?

To do this you may wish to bring your attention to your heart center. From this place, notice how your heart wants to relate to and feel about your body. We're often much kinder to our bodies when we bring compassion and love to them. When you experience this sense of connection, note it and take a moment to breathe that feeling into your whole being.

Then ask your mind, "What would be a positive and empowering way for me to think about my body?" See what comes to mind. Check whether this thinking is positive or whether you need to do more work. For example, if you get an answer from your mind that says, "I hope that in the future I'm thinner!" say "No!" to that. What you are seeking here is unconditional love and acceptance for your body. So, a positive reframe of the above statement could be: "I cherish you and trust that as we create a strong and powerful team. We will find a way for you to be strong and healthy." Notice how this statement engages your body and invites it into an active collaboration for the benefit of your 'whole': mind, body, heart and spirit.

What you are seeking is an experience where your mind, heart, body are connecting and having a dialogue. Trust that your essence and spirit will also emerge. And if not, finish the practice reflecting on what it is, what it was and what you'd like it to be.

What follows is a loving-kindness meditation that is a great way to cultivate a respectful and caring relationship with your connected whole-self. Being more fully connected within and practicing self-love will deeply enrich you, help you relate more smoothly with other people in your life and help you achieve what you want with ease, wisdom and grace.

LET'S TALK: 5 ACTIVITIES TO KICKSTART A CONVERSATION WITH YOUR BODY

## LOVING-KINDNESS MEDITATION

**Time:** 10-15 minutes

**You will need:** a quiet space and access to the audio recording of this meditation at www.maketimecount.com/media

**Time:** 10min

*"If I am not for myself, who will be for me?*
*If I am not for others, who am I?*
*And if not now, when?"*
Rabbi Hillel

What is Loving-Kindness Meditation?

Loving-kindness meditation, also known as Metta Bhavana, is a method of developing compassion and wise love. In this meditation, you will hone the skills of self-care, care and concern for others and greater tenderness – and you will have the opportunity to feel the warmth that comes when our heart and mind truly open. The practice comes from a Buddhist tradition and generally consists of silent repetitions of benevolent and good-willed phrases such as "may you be happy" or "may you be free from suffering" which are directed towards oneself and other people. This meditation helps develop your capacity for empathy and compassion.

We have known for some time that when we observe the emotions of others, parts of our own emotional circuitry used to create the same emotional state is triggered in our minds. Can we activate those same circuits voluntarily? Can we train ourselves to become more empathetic and kind?

Dr Richard Davidson, psychiatry and psychology professor at University of Wisconsin-Madison and his team addressed this question by comparing the brain activation patterns in Tibetan monks and novice meditators using fMRI[13] during loving-kindness meditation. In this elegant experiment, the researchers were able to examine what happened in the brain when feeling compassion.

The imaging showed that meditators showed greater activation in areas such as the insula, which helps the brain stay aware of our internal felt experience, as they practiced being compassionate.

---

13 Lutz A, Brefczynski-Lewis J, Johnstone T, Davidson RJ. (2008). Regulation of the Neural Circuitry of Emotion by Compassion Meditation: Effects of Meditative Expertise. PLOS ONE 3(3): e1897. https://doi.org/10.1371/journal.pone.0001897

Many other studies show the benefits of regular loving-kindness meditation, including stress reduction, slowing of aging by reducing the rate at which telomeres (the endpoints of our chromosomes) deteriorate, reduction in chronic pain, lowering severity of PTSD. Apart from these health benefits, loving-kindness meditation calms the body, increases levels of empathy and self-love and reduces our negative bias and negative feelings toward others. Of all the various forms of meditation, this one seems to benefit our general wellbeing, helps relieve some illnesses and has the potential to boost our ability to connect emotionally with other people.

Knowing what we know about the brain's inherent plasticity, we can strengthen our ability to empathise and feel positive emotions just as we are able to train sensory and motor skills. As we engage in an activity to activate specific neuronal circuits, those nerve cell connections strengthen. The more we do it, the stronger these connections become and we begin to reconnect to our bodies and the wisdom within them.

**Loving-Kindness Meditation Step-by-Step**

In order to be more loving towards our bodies, it makes sense to boost our capacity for compassion and kindness in general. My clients who learn and practice this meditation are noticeably kinder to themselves. Instead of allowing their internal critic to lash out at themselves over a temporary setback or punishing their bodies until they burn out, these clients achieve a more balanced and nurturing approach that brings mind and heart together. This way of being and working seems to produce good results, leaving them happier than when they first arrived, experiencing frequent mind and heart conflict.

- To begin, spend a few moments in preparation:

- Sit comfortably on a chair with your feet flat on the floor, your spine straight.

- Relax your whole body while remaining present to it.

- Place one or both of your hands on your heart and bring your awareness into your body.

- Take a few deep breaths in this position, inhaling and exhaling with calm and love for your entire being.

- Close your eyes and keep them closed throughout the mediation. Your meditation falls into four parts. You will wish yourself and others happiness and freedom from pain. You can listen to this meditation at www.maketimecount.com/bodytalk/media.

1. When you feel a connection with your body, repeat the following mantra silently three times:

   "May I live with ease, may I be happy, may I be free from pain." You may also hum it under your breath. What counts is the purity of your intention.

2. Picture someone you know (or have known) who you feel loves you very much. They may be alive or may have passed away. Imagine them sitting next to you on your right. Send all your love and best wishes to them by repeating the same mantra towards them three times:

   "May you live with ease, may you be happy, may you be free from pain".

3. Now picture another person who loves you sitting on your left. Repeat the same mantra sending your love and kindness to them:

   "Just as I wish this for me, may you be safe, may you be healthy, may you live with ease and may you possess complete happiness."

4. Now picture a person (or people) you do not know personally, but who may need support at this moment. Set an intention to send them love and kindness repeating the following mantra three times:

   "Just as I wish to be healthy and whole, may you live in good health, ease and happiness".

When you're ready, open your eyes and notice how you feel in your mind, heart, body and spirit. You have completed the loving-kindness meditation

Aim to practice this meditation as often as possible. I aim for once a week at least.

What we've learned so far

*"When you love someone, the best thing you can offer is your presence. How can you love if you are not there?"*
Thich Nhat Hanh


I hope you enjoyed learning more about you and your relationship with your physical body. What my work repeatedly teaches me is that connecting mind, heart, body and spirit creates brilliance and a fertile soil for whatever grows from here. When people connect within, it enables them to act with integrity and realize their potential without sabotaging their health, their principles or their values. As you become more integrated you will be able to serve yourself, others and the world with confidence, authority, resourcefulness, creativity and wisdom.

If you wish to return to any of the activities in this section and would appreciate using my guided audio recordings, visit www.maketime-count.com.

This is what I wish for you as we dive into the Body Talking.

# LET'S GET BODY TALKING

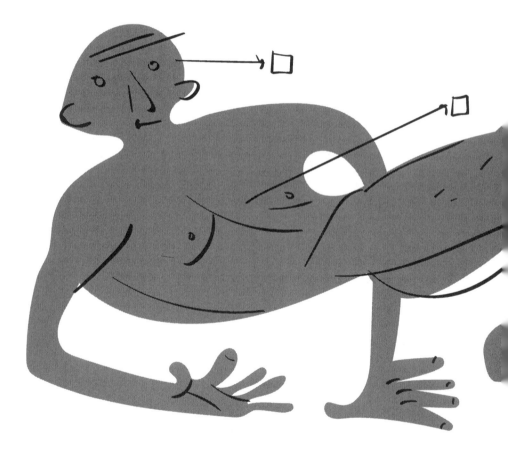

## Let's Get Body Talking

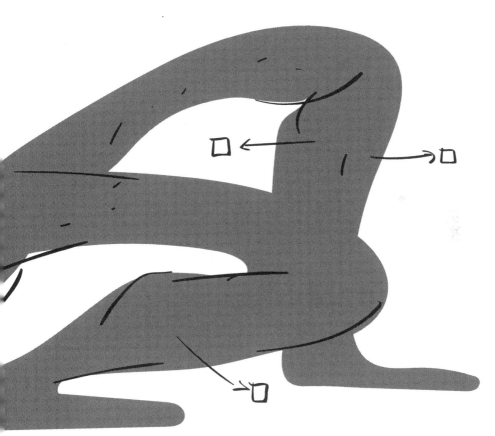

## New friendship with your physical self starts here

Body Talk is a fantastic way of reconnecting you with your physical self. It is the practice of enquiring within, with openness and curiosity and without fear, in order to marvel at what is revealed. Such a connection creates a state of wisdom and wholeness achieved as we integrate mind, heart, body and spirit. Such integration is the essence of my work and how it serves human empowerment.

Making this connection means embracing and 'owning' our being, a state that transcends cynicism and judgment – a mindset of simply 'being' with our physical body. It's a non-judgmental way of loving ourselves that can be witnessed in the innocence of children. Often it is the elderly who have the wisdom to appreciate the richness of life because of their life's experience. They often value the simple moments of life far more, living them with their whole being. Let's learn from both children and the elderly and let's enrich and broaden our experience of the present moment and our lives as a whole using that wisdom.

Many of us initially struggle with this process of inquiry because our mind senses that it's being unseated: its authority is being challenged by a deeper and more truthful inner wisdom. When you start Body Talking, it's not uncommon to hear your inner voice say "What's the point?" or "This is just make believe!" Don't be put off: persist and something deeper will be revealed - a new intuitive truth that the mind has probably been working hard to suppress or obscure from view.

Think of Body Talking as a self-loving commitment to allow your inner voice to surface. When this happens, the mind can do what the mind excels at: make sense of it and integrate it into everything else. In this process the heart, the spirit, the mind and the body begin to work together as one, realigning and transforming what is into what needs to be to serve you.

Here's my step-by-step guide to learning Body Talk and making it a habit – just like brushing your teeth.

## Body Talk method

**Time:** between 3 and 30 minutes depending on the Body Talk practice you choose.

There are three methods outlined in this book with links to audio recordings that will give you a place from which to start. You will most likely adapt them to fit your specific circumstances and/or, with time, your Body Talk practice will evolve to fully suit you.

In this section, I invite you to familiarise yourself with the general method so that you have a clear idea of the overall process.

Things to have for your Body Talk practice:

1. Time and space

    Designate a length of time that you wish to devote to reconnecting with your body. Depending on the depth you wish to go to and the time you have available, Body Talking can take from just a few minutes to half an hour or longer. Find a way to remain undisturbed.

2. A pen and some paper or your journal

    You will use this to draw an outline of your body as we did before in Exercise 3 (pg 103). You can do this to record what your body tells you and also any specific commitments you wish to make to your body in order to strengthen your new partnership (as we did in Exercise 4, pg 107).

3. A candle, fresh flowers, soft music, incense or music

Choose items that, for you, signify an openness to connect with your spiritual presence and spiritual guidance.

4. Comfortable clothing and a blanket

   The blanket serves two purposes: it supports your body in being comfortable and relaxed and it also supports the nervous system by providing comfort and helping alleviate any fear of what may emerge as you begin to practice.[14]

5. Love and positive regard for your whole being

6. Purity of intention

---

14 Our bodies regularly take input from the rest of the body and when it comes to our core embodied sense that helps us stay safe, the sensation of pleasant warmth associates with comfort that the body can sense in a way it can't feel words or a thought. The core reason for this is that the somatic nervous system (SNS) that innervates the skin, our sensory organs and all of the skeletal muscles is largely under conscious control. If I choose to touch something pleasant, or hug a person to obtain comfort during stress or stretch my tense muscles, I can bring about the effect I desire to have. As the SNS communicates with the autonomic nervous system (ANS), which is largely not under our conscious control but impacts our sense of calm and optimal function through its sympathetic and parasympathetic arms, the ANS will also start to regain more balance if it is either too revved up (where sympathetic action is dominant) or too chilled out by the countering parasympathetic action. Thus the first step in communicating with our entire system as mind, heart, body, and spirit is to help all parts achieve a state of safe and conscious engagement.

*131*

## Body Talk: Your Step-by-step Guide

Please read the instructions thoroughly at least once before you embark on your practice. As mentioned earlier in the book, you may also find it helpful to listen to the audios that will guide you through these practices. Visit www.maketimecount.com/bodytalk/media

Alternatively, you can record the instructions below onto your own device. This will allow you to play them back to guide you through the process using the power of your own voice. After just three or four sessions, the steps will become second nature and you will be able to complete your Body Talk sessions unaided. Regular practice and knowing your processes is valuable as it allows you to go at the pace at which your body is prepared to talk to you with no need to pause a recording, which can interfere with your session.

1. Set up

    - Gather your props (journal or paper, pen, candle, blanket) and find a comfortable place to sit. I often encourage clients to use a pillow and to sit on the floor supported by the sofa or a wall, but you may also sit on a sofa or seat – wherever you are most comfortable.

    - Light your candle or create what you need to allow you to mark the spiritual nature of your Body Talk.

2. Draw your body

    As spontaneously as possible create a body map. Allow your hand to draw a representation of your physical body. Trust that your hand knows how to do this and don't allow your mind to interfere by asking questions or evaluating what is produced.

It does not matter what the drawing looks like. Drawings from my own practice are scattered throughout this book to give you an idea. What's key is that you don't become hung up on this step. The drawing is simply an aid for recording your mind-body dialogue. You can draw both front and back of your body if you wish, although I often simply annotate my drawing to note whether an area from my back is speaking. You will find a general drawing on pg 152. Feel free to experiment.

3. A few moments of calm connection

- Put your drawing to one side, close your eyes and tune into your body. Begin by paying attention to your breath. Imagine your hand drawing a wave that mirrors your breath in depth, inhaling and exhaling. Do not attempt to control it. Do not judge it. Simply be present, noticing what it is like without needing to change it.

- Allow your muscles to relax - give them permission to ease back. Notice the feeling as they soften whilst still supporting you. Repeat this process at least three times to deepen your relaxation.

- Allow your mind to relax and 'melt' or 'drop' into your heart allowing your attention to settle away from any thoughts and into the feeling of love and self-acceptance that dwells here. Allow the loving sensation in your heart to spread throughout your body. Gently and slowly become inwardly curious and receptive as if you were tuning a radio to its best frequency.

4. Begin your Body Talk

You will find three examples of guided Body Talks on pg 155. Select one of them to follow or head over to www.maketimecount.com/bodytalk/media to download the audio versions. Whether you download my audio guides or attempt your own exploration, begin by applying conscious attention to simply being with your body. Don't try too hard. Simply breathe and tune inwards - make yourself available for your body to speak to you. Stay open and curious to the experience. Notice whether your attention and focus seem guided to any specific place or area. For example, you may sense a desire to start with your feet or the top of your head or your ears or an internal organ. If this happens, start there. If not, start with any part of the body and follow a pattern that suits you best. For example, you can start with:

- Your toes, working upward through the front of your body, to the head and then down through your back, ending at the soles of your feet.

- The front of your head to the back, move to the neck and shoulders front and back and work your way down to your feet.

- Your abdomen, working in circles outwards through your front and then your back.

- Your skin, working inwards through your organs and body sections: legs, arms, torso, head.

   Be willing to be guided by your body and your intuition; trust the process and your body's intelligence. There is no right or wrong place to start and finish. Equally, the depth and detail of your Body Talk, however it unfolds, will be right for you. You can of course experiment with techniques later but for now, it is more important to make a start with your practice. The audios to get started can be found at www.maketimecount.com/bodytalk/media. A full transcript example of a longer Body Talk practice is presented on pg 163

Tips on tuning-in and what to do if you encounter silence.

- Wherever you begin, turn your full loving attention and awareness to this area and simply become present to what is revealed. You may encounter silence, insight, advice, or a request. Ask the area you are focusing on what it needs, how it is, or if it has anything to tell you. Then simply stay present and see what arises. Trust that each part of your body is there to serve you and has vital information, wisdom, insights and ideas about what is good for you and what you truly need. Your job is simply to listen.

- At first it is very usual to not hear very much. If this happens, take a few deep, slow breaths and remain patient. Imagine your body is a shy animal. This is often the case for people who habitually take their bodies for granted and have lost connection with them. People who tend to think too much and find it hard to switch off may find this to be the case at the start. However, with practice, your dialogue will improve. If you encounter silence you may want to speak to this area of your body in a soft, loving voice and simply acknowledge that you're present and willing to listen.

- If, after some time, you still hear nothing or there is no new awareness, truth or requests coming from your body, send loving energy to this part and move to the next. Every Body Talk is different - you may hear back from many areas, from some or none.

5. Closing gratitude

When you have visited each part of the body that feels appropriate, complete the practice with a short statement of gratitude to your body. Here are some examples, but feel free to find your own:

- Thank you for being my physical body. I love you and I am grateful to you for being here to support me.

- Thank you for carrying me around and being my vessel. I am here because you of you.

- Thank you for serving me. I love and deeply respect you.

- Thank you for talking to me. I promise to remain respectful of you and keep listening to your truth.

6. Recording your Body Talk discoveries

- As you open your eyes, take your body drawing and make notes from your Body Talk practice. Just as you did during your practice, visit each part in turn and write on your drawing what you discovered there. Leave blank or write 'silence' on the parts that were silent.

- Mark any requests from your body that arose, with an 'action' symbol such as a star or tick box, so that you can return to these areas and tick them off when you've actioned your body's wise recommendations.

- Do not worry that you may have forgotten something crucial. Trust that what you have remembered is what needs to be remembered and acknowledged.

- Lastly, date the drawing for future reference. With more practice, you can record what your body says on your drawing during your practice. For those new to Body Talk practice, I recommend that you record what you have heard at the end of the session.

7. Bringing it all together

Look again at your drawing and revisit all the specific requests and comments that arose from your body. What's being divulged about the state of the relationship you currently have with your physical self? Make an overall promise to treat these insights with great respect and to help your body help you. Remember, the goal of your Body Talk practice is to rediscover and deepen the natural dialogue between your body and your capable, creative mind so that you are able to integrate your mind, body, heart and spirit. The greater goal is to help you self-realize without negating, harming, overstretching or undervaluing your physical self. Before you start your next Body Talk, you may wish to revisit your notes from your previous session. If you have answered any of the requests you received, make a note of these. Having a quick glance at your previous Body Talk can also quickly reveal the parts of the body that were active. Whether you do the review before or after your next session, the key point is to review the work to see how the dialogue and the narrative is evolving. For example, you may discover that more body parts speak to you, or sometimes less. You may notice persistent requests that you are not meeting or that lessen in intensity or even grow louder. Treat all of this as useful information.

# The 9 key principles of the Body talk

1. Trust

Body Talk is your invitation to deep knowing. A practice where you are guided by senses within you rather than your rational mind. It is not about evidence. On the contrary, it is about having faith. Trust requires that you begin your practice without knowing what the outcome will be and yet stay willing and open to experience whatever you hear.

In time, this trust will reward you with a new respect for your physical body and its true wisdom. As psychiatrist Bessel A. van der Kolk writes in his bestselling book *The Body Keeps the Score:* "The body does speak if we only dare to listen". Allowing ourselves to be guided is a means of rediscovering the power of the integrated self. When we are no longer hostages to one part's needs - often this part being the mind - we are able to serve our total self and produce better outcomes.

2. Relaxing into oneself

Being able to unwind is crucial for our mental and physical health. When muscles are tense, the physical body is wired for a response. This often means the 'fight and flight' pathways - physiological reactions in response to a perceived threat - are actively blocking higher brain areas from functioning fully. We have evolved to escape danger - spending time deliberating could mean the difference between staying alive and becoming prey.

Our instinctual fear responses operate largely outside of our conscious awareness precisely so that they can be deployed quickly. The part of the nervous system called the sympathetic nervous system gets us ready for threat with physiological reactions such as dilated pupils, increased heart rate and mobilised muscles. After the threat has passed, the parasympathetic nervous system helps the return to natural equilibrium by reactivating the 'rest and digest' responses: decreasing breathing and heart rate and supporting digestion.

Without relaxation, proper concentration is difficult – creativity and resourcefulness is hampered. Relaxation that leaves you alert, balanced, focused and yet refreshed comes from the active process of training your body and mind to align within. The physiological changes that happen as you relax act like little doses of immediate healing. Slow and deep breathing delivers more oxygen into the body, aiding sleep, which is hard to achieve if feeling wired or threatened. Relaxing muscles eases tension, which also sends feedback to the brain that it is safe.

3. Patience

Many traditions talk of patience as a virtue and it is something that few people are naturally good at. Today's world seems dominated by impatience. The word patience comes from the Latin root 'pati', which means to endure and bear. Patience develops alongside wisdom. The ego humbles when we face the fact that we have control over very little. Patience is a strength and developing your ability to be patient will raise your resilience and ability to cope with many challenging moments in life.

Patience also brings numerous rewards. Those who are patient often make better decisions, are more successful, make better use of time, connect more deeply within themselves and with others. They are better able to recover from difficulty and grow in wisdom. Patience is also related to love, which is explained further below.

4. Love of and for yourself

Self-love, and its cousin self-care, are much needed and often neglected practices. Many loving and caring people often do more for others but, in the process, short-change and neglect their own wellbeing. Self-love – or having deep respect and love of self – is vital for giving and sharing love with others. We can't give what we do not possess. How can I care for you if I am not in touch with what my own body and heart long for? It is impossible.

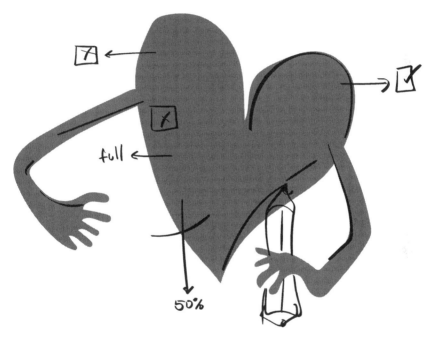

5. External expression through drawing

All forms of self-expression are healthy as they are a vehicle for witnessing and capturing our being at any given moment. If it is done with playfulness and lightness, drawing our form becomes part of a mindful practice of acknowledging our existence and a celebration of the freedom we have to express ourselves. No wonder every artist (and all human beings since the beginning of time) carry a strong desire to express and mark their existence long after they are gone.

In Body Talk, we tap into this practice and, by being spontaneous, we allow the more intuitive part of ourselves a voice. In this way, we reverse the general trend for the rational narrative to dominate.

6. Dialogue

I can't understate how important dialogue is as a means of giving ourselves and others the time, respect and reverence we all deserve. Effective communication is the foundation to everything. A key element of communication is the ability to listen. In Body Talk, we make space to hear our body's perspective and we train ourselves to listen better. This assists the practice of patience and non-judgmental acceptance and helps us to work with what is revealed in relation to the body rather than dominating it as if we know better! It helps us slow down, become more deliberate, curious and less fearful of what we may hear, not just during our Body Talk but in our other relationships as well.

7. Record keeping

Since time immemorial, human beings have felt compelled to record their thoughts, ideas, feelings and their very existence via every medium imaginable. Record keeping is a cornerstone of our lives and we have invented all kinds of systems - diaries, notebooks, pictures, record collections, recipes, journals, markings, engravings, even tattoos - to help us remember significant life events such as birth and death as well as everyday activities.

With Body Talk, keeping a record via your body drawings serves three specific functions:

- It documents the relationship you have with your body.

- It allows you to track how things are changing.

- It becomes a coaching and therapeutic tool allowing you to set goals and review progress.

8. Commitment

A commitment is a kept promise. We make commitments as a signal to others and to ourselves that something is of value to us. Keeping commitments is a foundation for developing trust, a key ingredient in building any well-functioning relationship. In fact, you could say that trust is simply the result of steadfast commitment kept over time. When commitments with our body are broken, our physical body learns that we are unreliable i.e. we can't be trusted. A rift between the mind and body occurs when the mind pushes the body around. Working together, mind and body are the ultimate power couple. Distrust and dissociation, however, disempower the whole.

## 9. Review and reflection

As Prof Eric Kandel, the renowned psychiatrist and developmental neurobiologist, who won the Nobel Prize in 2000 for his work on memory writes in his latest book *The Disordered Mind,* "Learning and memory are two of the most wondrous capabilities of our mind". Everything we know we have had to learn, and this can only be achieved by a process of functional memory involving storage of this knowledge over time. Our brains constantly create and revise memories, stringing them into a cohesive narrative of reality. A key marker of aging is a declining memory.

Because of the way memory works, learning and growth need conscious review and regular reflection. Going over what we have learned helps us make sense of the new truths and strengthens neuronal connections in the short-term. However, for information to convert into long-term memory, we must actually create new connections within the brain, i.e. we need to 'rewire' existing brain circuits and form new ones. The process of reflecting and recalling things strengthens synapses and as we reflect and fit new information into the existing fabric of what we already know, the anatomy of the brain changes.

Until a memory passes from a short-term memory to a more stable form of long-term memory, the new knowledge is not assimilated into our reality. In fact, paying conscious attention helps us associate what goes with what and make predictions and inferences we can test to aid how we learn. Ivan Pavlov conducted a famous experiment teaching dogs to salivate at the sound of a bell by pairing the sound with food, and thus creating a new association in the dog's brain. Humans too constantly make similar associations. During our Body Talk practice, we want to make our associations explicit by writing them down and reviewing them so that what we sense can form the basis that guides our behaviour.

It may be tempting to skip the last stage of your Body Talk, where you consider what arose, but this is a vital part in which you invite your mind to actually step in and help you take control of, and responsibility for, your new awareness. This is also why I encourage clients to review their past Body Talk practices, either before or immediately after they complete the next one. This helps note progress and integrate into the conscious knowing.

## Quick recap!

- Body Talk is a practice that helps you connect your physical body with your mind, heart and spirit.

- It is achieved through placing deliberate attention on different parts of your body in order to listen to the perspective, intelligence and truth arising from each area.

- Regular Body Talk dialogue helps cultivate a deeply respectful connection between mind and body, which can support what you wish to create in the world and get the best out of who you are.

- You are first and foremost your body. Distanced from it, you cease to 'feel' life. Without it, you cease to exist.

- Body Talk will help you become more 'whole', more integrated and it will benefit your physical, mental, emotional and spiritual health.

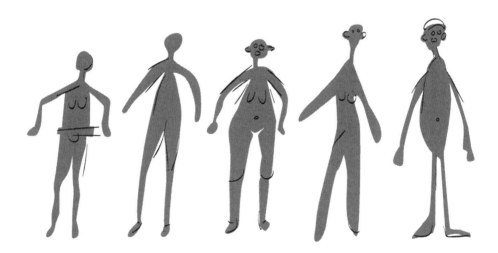

Developing Your Practice
Over 3 Months

## Creating your 3-month schedule

> *"I appreciate my life-giving heart, my beautiful mind, my lungs, muscles and bones and every organ. I appreciate the miracle of my physical body"*
> Daily affirmation

When it comes to trying something and seeing whether it can work, I am a fan of the three-tries approach.

1. First time – Experience Body Talk. Do it once to have a go.

2. Second time – Progress beyond your first try.

3. Third time – Begin to experience what it feels like to go beyond the basics.

I admit that this is not based on any scientifically proven method, but on my experience as a practitioner and through my own use of Body Talk. Three tries stands the test of time for me and three data points is a minimum one needs to detect a possible pattern.[15] If you are new to the Body Talk practice, I suggest aiming to complete one Body Talk activity per month over three consecutive months. This way what is discovered on your first Body Talk will have time to work its way through your conscious and subconscious mind, allowing you time to make small adjustments to how you approach life and how you look after yourself. As you manage to fulfil some of the requests your body makes or even follow gentle hunches from the practice about what you truly need, these incremental changes will be working

---

[15] I once developed a checklist tool to increase the quality of research proposals as part of an intensive developmental programme to grow the skills of professional scientists. Empirical testing showed that it took on average three people to agree on something before we could conclude that the answer was not simply an individual opinion but rather a small trend or tendency.

in the background towards a larger shift in how you self-care. Like chipping away at a stone, they will transform what happens in your mind, your emotions, how you feel physically and what is happening in your spiritual dimension. It's a belief I hold dear that one can achieve positive change through short, simple practices that are easy to weave every day into the fabric of who we are. After three months, I would expect you to be able to see the difference for yourself.

The three-month approach to testing and making new habits is based on how I coach clients in other areas of my work. I have found it to be the optimum length of time to bring about lasting change. I use it in my Grid framework[16] where I help people achieve greater fulfilment through work-life balance, with writers helping them create the first draft of their work.

One of the most frequent obstacles to a new practice is finding the time to implement it. In this section, you will find three separate Body Talk exercises: a quick session for when you have less than five minutes, a ten-minute medium-depth scan and a longer half-hour practice.

Which of the three Body Talk options to choose first is up to you. However, I suggest that you start with the one that you feel best suits your circumstances.

If you're time short, start with Body Talk 1: The Quick Session (three minutes). If you want to give yourself more time on your first attempt, you may wish to start with Body Talk 3 (30 minutes). Obviously you can vary this on your second, third and fourth practices, or you can repeat the three-minute session.

---

16 You can find out more about the Get Productive Grid via my website www.maketimecount.com or by getting a copy of my book by the same name.

DEVELOPING YOUR PRACTICE OVER 3 MONTHS

How often should you practice?

As I previously mentioned, aim for three separate Body Talk sessions in the first three months. This number of sessions will reveal a great deal. Try to set aside enough regular time to complete a full Body Talk (option 3) every four weeks. If you can't spare that amount of time don't miss out; choose a shorter practice instead. Whichever practice you opt for treat it as vital you-time, a self-caring and replenishing ritual. If you do more than three Body Talks in the three-month period that's fantastic! You will find your own rhythm and cycle as you try the Body Talk in practice.

Keep track of how your body feels in your journal or diary. Give yourself a daily vitality score, getting into the habit of keeping your body's needs in mind as you get on with your daily agenda. Imagine it as a practice of checking- in with your best friend to explore what you can accomplish together in way that supports you both.

Remember try to avoid rationalising or trying hard to understand what is revealed. Instead simply practice listening. One can talk and write about something to the nth degree but, in the end, what is learnt most is from is our own experience. With this in mind, dive in.

You're now ready for your three-month immersion in the Body Talk.

If you have done a Body Talk before don't forget to:

- Review your previous Body Talks to ensure you're building a richer awareness of your body and your relationship with it.

- Remember the commitments you made to your body or any requests that came from your body. Tick them off on your body drawing when they are completed.

- Think of your body as another person. If you don't make any time for your relationship with it, how will you possibly know it – and know yourself? Your body is your primary way of experiencing life. Dedicating some of your conscious awareness to your body yields many rewards.

Often what we need most to get started is a plan.

Your plan doesn't need to be fancy

All plans begin with the first step. Put a date in your diary for your first practice.

When you've completed your first practice, diarize the next date to practice.

Stick to this over the three months and you will notice clear benefits.

## Body map

This drawing is inspired by one of my favorite artists Pablo Picasso. If you are short on time or confidence to make your own Body Map, you can copy or use this drawing to make the notes from your practice.

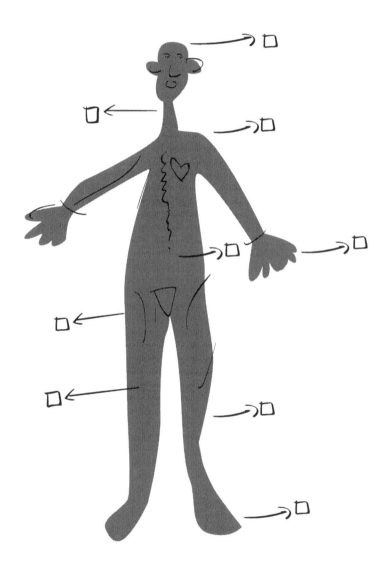

## Note-taking Checklist

To aid your practice over the next three months make a note of the following:

- ◊ Dates of your Body Talk practices

- ◊ 2-3 adjectives describing how you're feeling before starting, e.g. exhausted, gloomy, relaxed, calm, energised

- ◊ Body Map to note key findings – either one that is spontaneously drawn or one from this book.

- ◊ Any commitments to action(s) with a tick box to be able to note what was achieved when you return to the work to review in the future

- ◊ Gratitude statement: 1-3 sentences noting what you're most grateful for now.

- ◊ Exit state: 2-3 words capturing how you feel after completing your Body Talk

Use this checklist each time you prepare to practice Body Talk.

# 3 BODY TALK OPTIONS

# 3 Body Talk Options

3 BODY TALK OPTIONS

# BODY TALK 1: When time is short

**Time:** less than 3 minutes

Often it can seem like there is simply too much to do. The practices described below are super short and very effective. They will help you fit your Body Talk sessions into your life even when you are very busy.

There are six different quick Body Talks to choose from. Each one offers a quick way of checking in with your body, a Body Talk that can be done any time of the day, anywhere. Simply tune in to your physical body through any of these six entry points.

1. Focus on your abdomen - the center of your physical being.

Many physical manifestations of wellbeing (or lack of) start here, when the stomach and/or bowels are unwell.

What does it feel like inside this area?

You may sense for temperature, movement (or lack of movement, colour, general sensations and feeling, etc.

2. Check the energy level of your feet.

They carry you to action. Are they tired, restless, excited, achy, and motionless? Allow your feet to tell you how this feeling connects to your life or what is represents?

3. Scan for the energy and vitality in your body as a whole.

Rank your level of energy and vitality on a scale of

1 (very low) to 10 (very high).

Note where within your body you are able to detect the highest level of energy. Conversely, notice where you feel the least amount of energy and vitality, or perhaps none. Understanding your inner 'aliveness' will give you a good insight into your physical wellbeing.

If you have time, return to the place showing the highest energy and focus your attention here. Set an intention to help it disperse to other parts of your body that can benefit from it.

Take a deep long breath in and exhale any tension or worry that remains.

4. Become aware of any areas that present pain or discomfort or that simply feel different to your normal or best.

For example, you may be more aware of your ears because they are hot

or the joint in your left hand which aches, making you flex your finger.

Allow the knowledge of the cause of this to surge from this location towards your mind. Note any insight, hunch, advice or request.

With practice, your ability to sense your physical body will improve.

5. Ask your body to complete the following statements and simply allow it to answer for itself.

a. As a whole, my body currently feels _____.

b. What my body needs most right now is _____.

## 3 BODY TALK OPTIONS

    c. The part of my body that feels most centered and at peace is _____.

    d. The part of my body that feels agitated is _____.

    e. The part of my body that feels neglected is _____.

    f. Knowing what I know now, the one action I wish to take to improve on my present situation is _____.

6. Commit to one simple act of kindness that will support your body today.

This may include

rest,

sleep,

fresh air,

exercise,

meditation,

massage,

a bath,

giving or receiving a hug,

wearing favourite clothes,

basking in the sun,

playing with your pet,

savoring a piece of chocolate,

etc.

## BODY TALK 2: STANDING BODY TALK

**Time:** 10-15 minutes

Your physical body has nerve cells that constantly transmit what's going on – a memory being stored and recalled, a new one being formed. By tuning our attention inwards, we can start to sense and to interpret these experiences. This is the definition of aliveness: being present to the miracle of life taking place at every level of your physical being.

Our bodies speak to us in many ways. They speak with heat, color, movement, and degrees of presence and aliveness. In this practice, we will be looking and sensing the body from within.

Body Talk 2 practice is hugely beneficial as it takes you deeper, connecting with your body through posture, grounding with the earth and attuning to what is within you. It can be done at any time of the day.

1. Stand with your arms by your sides and your feet about 12 inches apart. Assume a strong, confident yet relaxed stance. You may wish to close your eyes or simply look ahead and soften your gaze.

2. Loosen or drop your shoulders. Feel the weight of your hands at your side. Push your weight onto the back of your heels and then onto the front of your toes to ground yourself. Tune into the gravitational support mother earth provides. Feel yourself extending upwards towards father sky. Take deliberate breaths but don't alter how you breathe. Simply attune to your breath flowing through your body oxygenating it.

3. Picture the path of your breath. Entering through your mouth or nose into your lungs and outwards to every tiny bit of your

physical body supplying life-energy to it. Imagine a loving exchange of life-giving oxygen with anything that no longer serves you, which you exhale. Breathe in life and positive sustenance and exhale waste. Do this approximately eight to ten times.

4. Notice the area of your body that holds strength. For example, you may find strength is present in your midsection, your chin, your forehead or in your chest.

5. Similarly, notice if there are any areas of your body where you feel weakness.

6. Become increasingly curious about your body. Pay attention to where you can detect a vibration or feeling. This could be tingling, numbness, excitement, an itching or even a blockage. It may be a sensation that is hard to describe but one which you can clearly sense. Without needing to name it, simply sense it. Note the location. You may find several, a few or none. You may also find that there is an energy that is evenly distributed throughout your body apart from one or two distinct areas. You may find your body buzzing with excitement or very calm and serene. Simply take the time to notice. The goal here is to purely connect with your physicality.

7. Now begin to scan your body. From the top of your head towards your feet or from your feet upwards, one specific area at a time. You may wish to start with your front, your back or scan both working your way up or down. For example, you could start with your head, paying attention to your scalp, forehead, eyes, ears, nose, back of your head, your chin, cheeks and your neck.

8. Ask each part of your body "What is true here?" as if you are checking in with each member of a team. You may get a response

*161*

from some areas or a visual image of this area at a cellular level. It is not uncommon to sense a playground, troops in trenches, a busy factory work floor, a protest march, a defiant crowd; to see or sense colour or perceive or even hear music or rhythm. Trust that whatever comes is good. Accept it without judging or intellectualizing it. If you get a sense that what you are hearing is coming from your mind trying to take control, simply relax, breathe calmly and deeply and try again.

9. Allow your consciousness to expand beyond what your mind knows or believes is possible. Allow yourself to imagine the various communication networks and highways connecting within you: your skeletal system, muscles, circulatory system, organs, autonomic reflexes, the sense organs (eyes, ears, nose, mouth, skin) as well as the intuitive and emotive channels that reflect and create your mental state. Attune your attention to them and see what comes to light.

10. Use your body drawing to record what you have discovered in this activity.

11. If you receive any requests, make a note of them on your drawing and make commitments to honor them over the coming days and weeks.

## BODY TALK 3: IN-DEPTH BODY TALK

**Time:** 30+ minutes

Whilst you will already be familiar with the general concept of Body Talk method, you may wish to try out the transcript below which comes from my guided Body Talk work with one-to-one clients. Reading it first will give you an idea how the exercise works, its key parts and how you may wish to adopt it for your personal and/or professional practice. You will find the audio recording at www.maketimecount.com/bodytalk/media. If you prefer listening to your own voice, you may like to record this yourself and play it back.

TRANSCRIPT

*Hello*

*This recording is designed to support you in your practice by giving you an example of a Body Talk activity you can use for yourself or facilitate for a client. This exercise will help you tune into and begin to work with your body in a true partnership where your body will support your actions.*

*Without the body the brain cannot function. In my work with clients I often find that it is the state of their existing bodies that gets in the way of what they wish to achieve and the lifestyle they wish to create. Thus, it is often a very good idea to begin at this level.*

*Make connecting with your body a ritual.*

*I light a candle close to me because I like to celebrate a sense of communion with my body; the same way one would when inviting a best friend over. I would encourage you to do the same.*

## 3 BODY TALK OPTIONS

*Establish internal calm.*

*Find a quiet and comfortable place where you can either lie down or sit comfortably. A space where you can devote time to focus on the journey you are going to take and the conversation you are going to have with your body.*

*You may hear me breathing. I'd like you to close your eyes and join me simply in breathing.*

*You may experience your breath, very much like an ocean wave. I'd like you to give it that quality, placing your full attention to what your wave of breath sounds and feels like as you inhale and exhale. Allow your breath to caress your inner body as you inhale to power your body and breathe it out to purify yourself. I'd like you to feel the calm that shows up as you caress your body with your breath, with life.*

*Take at least five long, deep, relaxed breaths.*

*Continue breathing long, deep, relaxed breaths and notice the lightness, or the shedding of weight as you take these breaths. Allow the energy of anything trapped in your body to simply be released on the wave of one of your exhalations. For example if you're feeling sadness, grief or are holding onto a problem in your mind, use your breath to move that energy through and feel yourself becoming freer as you breathe it out. Thoughts and emotions that get stuck in the body block energy. Breathing gently gets to work on those stuck points and helps you reconnect within.*

*Connect with your body from a mindful and consciously present place*

*Next I'd like you to continue with the long, deep, relaxed breathing and begin to tune your energy to your toes. As we move through your body pay particular attention to the different sensations in your body, and the messages that surface from the different parts in terms of what they, as vital components of your whole-self, need of you in order to be your best friend. Many times, in the busyness of daily life, we lose touch with our physical self. It is then that the vital messages about attunement, health and support that are given to us simply do not make it to our conscious awareness.*

*A Body Talk activity such as the one we are doing is a very simple and effective way to make time for our bodies and to make time for the inner senses in order to meet the commitments of supporting our full self in wellbeing. Therefore, as you tune into your toes, and perhaps wiggle them, let's really focus on them to see or sense what energy emanates from this region. Whatever answer appears is fine, including a sense of nothing. Let's now focus on our feet as a whole and see what they have to tell us about their needs. Note whatever message or information you receive and then move your focus to your knees. The knees, the most complex joints in our body, act as vital and complex suspension systems carrying us around, helping us move towards the very things we want and desire. Tune into these natural gears and hear what your knees say to you.*

*Move up to your hip area and, here again, tune into this region with care, compassion and readiness to hear what the hip area wants to share with you.*

*Now tune into your stomach. For many people this area and the gut carry and store a great deal of drama, tension, conflict and stress. Many people report a sense of regular bloating, tension and/or discomfort in this area. The stomach is often referred to as our 'core'. We talk about feeling things in 'the pit of our stomach' or in our gut when we feel scared, when we deeply love and when things truly touch us. Tune into this region, you may even wish to stroke your stomach, accept it for what it is.*

## 3 BODY TALK OPTIONS

*As you do this, listen for any messages or awareness coming from this part of your body. You may feel an insight arise or a sense of intelligence or advice. You may receive a request in terms of what your stomach area needs to help serve you best. Again, you may hear nothing, or you may receive specific instructions and requests from this part of your body.*

*Move up towards your chest area and the heart. Again, tune in to give this part of your body attention and to listen to what is going on here. What does this area look like? Is there a particular image that comes into your mind? What does it feel like? What do the cells in this body part want to tell you? Really listen with an open mind to hear the messages from this part of your body in terms of what it needs to help serve you best.*

*Now tune into your shoulders. The shoulders, for many, are the very physical place that literally 'shoulder' responsibilities, challenges, issues and the things that we feel we have to handle in life. This is another vital part of our body so tune in to see what your shoulders have to tell you. Sit back, breathe and open your internal awareness to any messages coming from this part of your body in terms of what it needs to help serve you best.*

*Move down your arms towards your elbows. For many of us our elbows often seem a hidden part of us. We don't necessarily pay much attention to our elbows, and yet just like the springs in our knees our elbows power our hands and aid our ability to make things in the world. Tune into your elbows and give them your attention and see what you notice in this area.*

*Move down towards your wrists and your hands. For me hands are the absolute magic of our body. In the same way that feet give us stability in placing us steadily on the surface of this earth, our hands are a direct energy channel. Everything we touch metaphorically and physically with our hands, including the food we put into our body, the people we physically come into contact with and the energy we leave in that connection, along with the things we dream of and eventually execute, whether that is at a typewriter, at a design desk or anywhere else, be it a lab bench or a home-office, will come from these wonderfully designed structures. Give them your full attention. You may wish to place your hands in your lap and open them in a gesture of receiving. Feel your hands, focus on their messages to you. What do your hands tell you that they need of you to help serve you best?*

*Remember to stay with your attention on each part of your body for as long as it takes to give them the full attention they deserve. Bear in mind that some of your body sections may not have had a chance for such a genuine dialogue in a very long time - perhaps not ever - and so, like a shy friend, it may take a little time and patience before it begins to open up and develop the trust that you will hear and act upon what is revealed to you to help serve you best.*

*Now put your hands to your heart and begin to feel a sense of alignment with your body. Take a moment to pause whilst doing this. Send love and gratitude to your heart and your body helping them connect for greater health and joy.*

*Now go up towards your neck area. This wonderful structure literally carries the weight of your head all the time except when resting and sleeping. See what your neck area, which for many people is a place of tremendous tension, including the source of headaches, reveals to you. Tune into your neck, tune into its base, its middle and to the back and front of it and see what you can sense and experience in this part of your body.*

*Now ascend higher to your mind, encased in your skull and in your physical brain. Start to enquire as you enter the beautiful mesh of nerve cells, signals and exciting nerve impulses flying through this space, what is needed here to create order and to help your mind to help serve you best?*

*Whilst in this region, I would also like to invite you to stay in your mind and to pay particular attention to the incoming requests from your sense areas such as your ears, nose, lips, your sense of taste and your eyes. Visit them in your own sequence and tune into each of them to see what they need. Stay quiet and listen for a good minute.*

*The messages I received from these body parts were as follows: my eyes made a request for seeing some trees in the forest. My sense of smell and my nose made a request for a lovely Italian meal that I would cook for my dear family and friends at one of our family gatherings. My lips made a request to hug and kiss my friends more often and make more time for those people and the magic of our connections. My ears made a request that I travel and expose them to a sense of a small country stream and the lovely noise that they find so calming and pleasing as I hear the water falling over the rocks. Whatever body messages you have received, just acknowledge and trust, they are just fine.*

*Another area - your upper back - is hugely important and often can be a place where tension is held and pain felt. Take a journey towards your upper back, your shoulder blades and the space between your spine and your upper back. What do you sense in this part? What is needed in this area to help serve you best?*

*Now move down towards your lower back and buttocks. This area is a major station for the nerves that reach and innervate your legs, the springs in your knees and your feet. The lower back connects your entire body and grounds it. It is often a large nucleus of tension, stored pressure, the result of which can cause problems. Yet your lower back can also be supple and fluid with practice. So, tune into that area now and begin to see what your lower back needs from you to help serve you best.*

*I feel a wonderful sense of space in my lower back. Surprisingly I have no pain which is somewhat unusual. I also feel a tremendous connection in my heart to you listening to this recording and what you are going to discover about your body and how it is serving you in your connection and communion with it. If you wish, you may want to pause this recording to visit other parts of your body, perhaps particular organs or sections, or to return to parts that were silent and give them another opportunity to speak their truth to you. Remember that whatever you hear is good as the answers to these needs will serve you well.*

*When the recording finishes take a piece of paper and draw a small figure representing your body. Write down all the different messages and requests you received on your drawing. You could also use the drawing provided in your Body Talk book (pg 152) for ease of use. As you write down your requests and commitments to your body, find a way to incorporate them into your life so that you give your body - your best friend - what it needs most in order to fully support your wellbeing in the pursuit of your dreams and in the realisation of the things you want to create and achieve in the world.*

*Take three more breaths, to center and close your Body Talk practice, trust deeply that everything you have heard, discovered and learned from your practice are the very things that you need at this moment in time to serve you well.*

*When ready simply open your eyes. Put a smile on your face knowing you have just given yourself the wonderful gift of really caring for and centring on your body.*

*Thank you for following this practice. I wish you health, vitality and a wonderful sense of wellbeing that permeates and restores every little area of your remarkable body, the physical sense of you that makes for that physical presence which is you.*

*Thank you for joining me and whenever you practice I wish you awesome, restorative sessions.*

## Frequently asked questions

1. Where in the body should I start my Body Talk?

You can begin wherever you are called to start, where you sense there is something that wants to talk, where you feel discomfort or pain. Or you can follow a specific routine as described in the in-depth Body Talk transcript. It matters not where you begin, where you end, or if you omit a part, simply trust the process. Your body is like your family. When some parts speak up but one specific part gets continuously neglected, this part will also speak up or even scream to obtain your attention. Have faith in your thoughts.

2. What if I don't get a response?

I have invited many clients to practice Body Talk. To begin with I would often encourage them to simply attune to what they felt whilst guiding them through a version of the in-depth Body Talk. Following this I would share with them the recording so they could practice on their own. It is not uncommon for some people to need a few attempts before they sense an internal response.

It can be easy to give up at an early stage from the discomfort of hearing mainly silence. This often simply means that the mind is blocking the process and impatience is getting in the way of a better result. Those who find the first few practices hard often battle with incessant thinking as they find it hard to switch off. The more we pay attention to the mind the more easily it is to undervalue the powerful way that our physical body also speaks. As a coach, I often find myself reminding my clients that if I felt neglected, I too would fall silent and take time before I'd speak. I encourage them to be patient and to persist with their practice. I offer you the same advice. Show

*171*

## 3 BODY TALK OPTIONS

up to this practice with complete love and compassion for yourself and leave aside all expectations and judgments.

Your Body Talk practice is a relationship-building activity. The relationship is between you and your physical body. Persist and be patient like the most loving parent, partner or carer. The more love and patience you show, the more you encourage the less prominent parts of yourself to take center stage and the more you will hone your listening skills.

3. When I get a response, is this not simply my mind taking control?

Yes, often the mind talks instead of the body but it sounds different. You will discover this for yourself with practice. Sometimes you'll hear what I call 'defensive jabber' from your controlling mind. This stems from a fundamental fear that it may find out things it might not be able to handle – to the total detriment of you. This can take the form of an instant opinion, evaluation or suggestion. When your mind speaks, you hear a thought. You will feel yourself occupied in your mind as it tries to interpret what's going on. Breathe and simply acknowledge this is happening. Tell your mind to relax and move aside. Tune into your body. Body awareness and wisdom will arise from within. It will feel highly intuitive and whilst your mind needs to translate this into language, the original message is more like a sense or insight. It can be in the form of an abstract sensation, a colour or an image. It is your mind that must stay patient and open to what will come to light and then tell you what it is.

Many times doing Body Talk with my clients and for myself, has revealed a painful yet vital truth that needed to be dealt with and that corresponded to a higher good. The mind blocked or drowned out this truth with jabber, explanations, rationalisations and even judgmental comments like "Oh what's the point of this?" or "This is such nonsense!" These defensive remarks are an attempt to block the natural process from continuing. This is why Body Talking is a gentle practice that requires your patience as it builds compassion for the ego in your mind.

4. What if I can't give my body what it needs?

There may be times when your Body Talk practice returns a request you feel you can't meet. For example, you may be single and without a partner when your body gives you the message that it craves or wants to feel intimacy. Or imagine that the image of a rainforest or desert sands comes up during your Body Talk. You don't have the time or the money to just take off for a trek through the Amazon or Sahara. In such a situation, note the request and really tap your mind for a creative way that you can respond to the request. This may require you looking deeper into the essence or values that are being sought within the request. Perhaps the request for intimacy is about being caressed and you can satisfy this request by booking yourself a full body massage. At the same time you could also begin to explore dating or connecting with others if this was something you were ready for. Similarly, an image or craving to be on a hot sandy beach or in a remote place may be a need for solitude or adventure.

The body is a natural lover. We love with our physical bodies and it is also how we sense physical love from others. Being a lover, the body is very understanding. If you don't believe this, simply observe the level of misuse the body tolerates before it rebels and says enough! Your body will love you simply for listening and trying your best. Where there is a will there is a way and your mind can be extremely creative when it wants to be. As your mind-body dialogue strengthens, your mind will listen and help your body feel more connected and involved in keeping you well.

## 3 BODY TALK OPTIONS

There will be some commitments that may take longer to fulfil than others. I often have commitments that take two or three additional Body Talks before I can go back to my drawing to mark that I have honored them. For example, it may be a few weeks before I can get away to the seaside to honor my commitment to my eyes, ears and nose (stunning sea views, the calming sounds of the waves on the shore and the cleansing fresh sea-air). However, in the meantime, I can occasionally immerse myself for a few minutes in an audio recording of the ocean waves and simply listen to how they crash on the shore. The key here is the intention and the respect we give to our bodies in making a commitment in the first place.

Remember, all requests from your body are invitations to connect with your deepest needs and longings. As you learn to give them a voice, you will find yourself more content, more balanced and more peaceful within. You will deepen your level of presence, attention and connection. This is a gift: a true miracle.

5. I feel disconnected from my body – as though I am outside of it

The body has the sensory capacity to provide us with a means of having feelings, be that through our lover's kiss or listening to a favorite song that gives us goose bumps. However, it is not uncommon to feel a sense of disconnection from our body, a sense of standing alongside your physical body or as though your body is somehow separate from you. This is what psychologists term dissociation: a form of conscious or unconscious disconnecting or separating from one's physical self. The cause of dissociation may be associated with trauma, acute stress or a fear of experiencing something that hooks into fearful responses from the past. This often happens during interactions where, instead of being with someone in what is – be that a date, an argument, a conversation, or just sharing silence – one or both people dissociate from the experience as if it's not real and begin to judge, evaluate, block or somehow distort it.

Dissociation is a coping mechanism that separates the person from an experience or a memory in order to avoid the experience. It can vary in strength depending on the degree of stress or threat experienced. For those who spend a great deal of time in their heads entertaining their thoughts, dissociation may go largely unnoticed yet be very real. I have found that an imbalance within us between mind, heart, body and spirit can result in dissociation, which may have deeper roots such as real trauma.

The bottom line is this: if you're not in your body, you can't be experiencing life! Therefore, any form of separation from your physical self will have a tendency to rob you of the richness of experience.

Here are a few possible signs that dissociation may be happening:

- Experiencing mental health problems such as depression and/or anxiety that persist for some time.

- A sense of detachment from one's physical body; feeling oneself outside the physical dimension or hovering above oneself.

- Feeling as if life is a movie one is watching instead of experiencing real life.

- Inability to sense or report specific feelings in the body.

- Unclear sense of who one is and/or how it feels to be you.

- Feeling or wanting to end one's life or questioning the point of life.

- Significant stress in life.

- A relationship (personal or work) that elicits fear.

- Presence of multiple voices in one's head or a sense of constant thoughts being present in the mind.

- Feeling dazed and confused.

- Sense of there being multiple identities within your body.

- Feeling as if you, or other people, are robot-like and inhuman.

Whilst we all disconnect from time to time and dissociation covers a broad spectrum, if any of the descriptions above capture how you feel much of the time or in specific situations, I would encourage you to speak to your doctor or seek counseling to explore the impact of this on you and your life.

I have found that Body Talk helps many of my clients regain their physical selves, discover and assume more authority and a fuller physical presence so that their experience of life grows in richness and depth and the way in which they connect with others is transformed.

# 3 Month Review

3 MONTH REVIEW

## How to know if the Body Talk is helping me?

You now have all you need to practice Body Talk, and you may have created your own unique practice. Allow this to keep developing.

This work is not easy. For those with patience and devotion to their own body, it will yield great depths of self-knowing, facilitate balance, which is key to a meaningful and fulfilling life.

The body is your foundation.

See how far you've come by repeating the initial activities (pg 46-119).

Notice the changes and what remains the same.

Write a note in your journal noting:

- What, if any, changes have occurred in your life and how you're feeling since you began?

- What remains the same?

- What else could change for the better and what will you have to do to make this happen?

Many clients who regularly practice Body Talk find that it becomes easier to hear the body speak in a voice that is distinct from what their minds would say. Some of the issues marked on your body map may have either diminished or gone away completely. Some areas might now be more able and willing to tell you their story. Most of all, you should feel more connected to your body as an integral part of who you are, something that experiences you and gives you constant feedback. You may feel more integrated or whole.

Many clients find that Body Talk helps them return to a more balanced life in which they are more mindful and attentive to their mental,

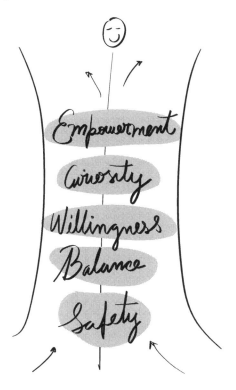

physical, emotional and spiritual health. It seems that whatever was not quite right in their lives – conflict, tension, frustration – as well as whatever was going well tends to surface during their Body Talk practice.

As they come face-to-face with this knowledge, many are deeply moved, in awe of the miraculous way that their bodies can help support their sense of agency and a feeling of empowerment. The more the mind, heart, body and spirit align, the more people act from their true center where their full power resides. This return to greater homeostasis, to calm, peace and full function, is what I believe underpins all wellbeing and facilitates best performance in us all

## Congratulations on getting reconnected

You did it!

Throughout your life your body should be your best friend and valued guide. Its physical limits provide a useful boundary which, when respected, will expand and strengthen.

Make Body Talk part of your regular practice of self-care. You may wish to make this a daily, weekly or monthly ritual depending on your specific needs and life circumstances. For example, as part of a maintenance practice, I perform a Body Talk practice every seven to nine weeks. However, there are times when the need to return to the practice simply arises within me. I listen to and obey this calling, make time for practice and make reference to it in my journal. Remember, what you're developing in this work is a new, effective dialogue and partnership with your physical body.

Speaking as someone with a chronic health condition, who needs to remember to keep my body's needs at the forefront of my mind, if you make space for your physical body to have a voice, you will benefit from its wisdom in many ways.

Here are just a few of the benefits:

- A greater sense of certainty that you're doing the right things.

- Feeling more at peace within.

- Greater presence and confidence.

- Feeling more grounded.

- A greater sense of pride and dignity from taking better care of yourself.

- A greater knowledge of, and appreciation for, yourself and your specific stage in life.

- A better understanding of how people can enhance your life.

- The ability to read situations and people with greater sensitivity and accuracy.

- A greater sense of all-round wellbeing and vitality.

If you wish to continue your work, you will find five additional activities you can do at any time in the last section of this book. These activities will deepen your mind-body connection and help you assess how much you have strengthened your overall mind, heart and body dialogue. Skim read them quickly to discover one that suits you best or the one that specifically calls out to you. The activities are from my workshops and retreats. They are intended to help you deepen your Body Talk work and aid you in noticing how far you have progressed through your Body Talk journey.

# 5 Additional Activities to Deepen Internal Connection

# 5 ADDITIONAL ACTIVITIES TO DEEPEN INTERNAL CONNECTION

## Introduction: Self-care is a vital practice and skill

Within the context of mental health and emotional wellbeing, self-care has become one of the most important activities in the last few years. As lives become increasingly busy, its importance will only rise. It is apparent that whilst we know about the importance of brushing our teeth and good daily personal hygiene, how to regularly care for our minds and hearts is often overlooked. And yet, being OK mentally, physically, emotionally and spiritually is the basis for everything else. This is especially true for many working in the helping professions, where high demands to stay well are placed; professions in healthcare, education, ministry and the service sector. The exercises in this section invite you to regain control and start looking after yourself!

# ACTIVITY 1: HELLO ME MIRROR EXERCISE

**Goal:** To develop or deepen a healthy relationship with yourself

**Time:** 20 minutes

**You will need:** a large mirror in which you can see your head and shoulders in a good light, a timer, journal and pen.

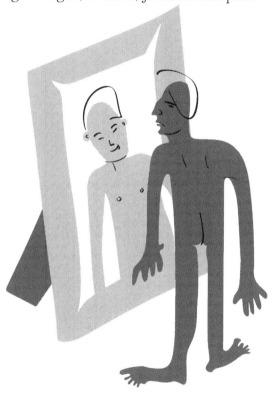

*"If you're searching for that one person
that will change your life
take a look in the mirror"*
Unknown

# 5 ADDITIONAL ACTIVITIES TO DEEPEN INTERNAL CONNECTION

Hello Me Mirror Exercise is one of my most beloved activities to share with clients. This one is a modified version of a cornerstone practice from my best-selling 30-day goal achieving online course with *Psychologies* magazine.[17]

## Instructions:

This exercise gets you to face yourself as you are and to begin to develop a relationship with all of you – the bits you may already know inside out and parts you under-focus on. It is also designed to discover layers of you that have more to reveal. It is a wonderful exercise for developing self-love, positive self-regard; building confidence and staying current with the person we're growing into with each day and moment.

Repeat this exercise once a week over three consecutive weeks. Each time do a slightly different version of the exercise to help get connected with your physical presence.

Week 1

1. Sit or stand in front of your mirror in silence*. Set your timer for 10 minutes and simply stare at your reflection in the mirror, notice what you see looking back at you. You are now in an intentional presence with yourself.

- Who is this person?

- What can you see in their face? For example does their face communicate worry, displeasure, joy, calm, satisfaction?

- Do you like the person you see?

17 You can access the course here https://www.psychologies.co.uk/how-supercharge-your-goal-setting

- Do you respect the person you see?

- Do you see the potential in the person you see? Or, do you only find fault in the person you see?

2. After 10 minutes, take few moments to write down a short description of what you saw. Start this with the following words: What I see right now is... See where this takes you. Save your written work for next week.

*I also recommend listening to Michael Jackson's Man in the Mirror song while completing this exercise. The philosopher Nietzsche observed, "We listen to music with our muscles". In other words, music is a powerful influencer of the mind.

Week 2

1. Stand or sit in front of your mirror in silence* and set your timer for 10 minutes. For the next ten minutes simply look at your reflection in the mirror and look for a 'hero' within you.

- What is it that you see looking back at you? For example you may notice that the face, demeanour and posture of the figure reflected in the mirror is one that embodies pride or courage. Perhaps it belongs to a person who is a survivor, artist, seeker, student, teacher etc.

- How does it feel to see yourself as a Hero?

2. Observe the emotions that arise as you search for your inner hero.

5 ADDITIONAL ACTIVITIES TO DEEPEN INTERNAL CONNECTION

3. What ordeals, trials, challenges or quests have they been though? Notice their strengths and vulnerabilities. What gifts have they collected through the journeys they have been on?

4. What ordeals, trials, challenges or quests are they on now?

5. When you finish, take few moments to write down your reflections. Save your written work for next week.

* I recommend listening to Search for the Hero by M People while completing this exercise.

Week 3

- Stand or sit in front of your mirror in silence*. As before, set your timer for 10 minutes. During this 10 minutes simply look at your own reflection with nothing but complete appreciation. Note the features that give you the most character and interest.

- Imagine you know nothing about the person looking back at you other than that they are simply fantastic! What would be your guess as to who is behind the vision? What they do? What's their story?

- Having detached yourself from how you normally view yourself, how does it feel to see your reflection in this way?

- When your time is up, make a note of your favourite feature or characteristic and pledge an intention to celebrate it and show it off. Wear yourself proud. Step into your dignity and simply be yourself.

\* Walking on Sunshine by Katrina and the Waves is the perfect musical accompaniment for this exercise.

What you may experience

On an everyday basis it is often the case that you rarely see yourself with true attention. During this practice what you will discover is someone worth knowing, worth loving, someone you can be proud of. You are a beautiful, original being and there is no other like you, with your foibles, insecurities, idiosyncrasies, your likes and dislikes, the things you wish were different. All this comes together to create you.

Isn't it time you embraced yourself with love, acceptance, encouragement and trust in your ever-growing potential?

What you are today is undoubtedly shaped by what you think and feel about yourself – so choose your thoughts and feelings wisely.

# 5 ADDITIONAL ACTIVITIES TO DEEPEN INTERNAL CONNECTION

## ACTIVITY 2: THE HARE & THE TORTOISE

**Goal:** To help find balance between your overachiever and your procrastinator.

**Time:** 20 min

**You will need:** 20 minutes undisturbed time alone

*"Every truth has two sides; it is as well to look at both, before we commit ourselves to either."*
Aesop

We live in a world that demands a certain pace of us. The premise of the modern world is this: do more and you will live more. However, living life at a fast pace rarely delivers on the promise of a better life. Paradoxically, it can often erode the quality and experience of life itself. To address this we need to develop the wisdom to judge when living fast helps but be able to identify when slow is better. In other words, what matters most is finding a balance.

Whether you're a driven overachiever (a hare) or a procrastinator (a tortoise), there is a bit of each in all of us – and that's a good thing.

One of the biggest obstacles to success, health, wellbeing and having good relationships is when our inner 'hare' energy (the part of us that wants to rush to the finish line) and our 'tortoise' energy (our slow and cautious side) are out of balance. Sometimes our 'tortoise' steps in when we need our 'hare' and vice versa. Remember, the person who oversees them is you! It is your choice when your tortoise takes the stage and when you unleash your hare. Stepping into this place of choice is where empowerment is found.

This exercise will help you really get to know the hare and tortoise in you and assign each of them suitable roles in your life, ensuring that the winner of any race is you.

This activity starts with the famous Aesop fable, which you probably read as a child. The version below is my retelling of it.

## 5 ADDITIONAL ACTIVITIES TO DEEPEN INTERNAL CONNECTION

*Once upon a time there was a very fast hare
who enjoyed boasting about his speed.
An old tortoise, who finally grew tired of hearing the hare bragging
challenged the hare to a race.
All the other animals became curious and turned up to watch the race.
When the starting gun was fired, the hare set off so fast
that when the dust settled the tortoise was barely over the starting line.
When the hare looked back and saw this, he laughed out loud thinking
"Silly tortoise! He can't expect to win the race moving at that speed!"
After running a while, the hare got bored and thought
"I'm so ahead, it won't hurt to pause a while and take a nap."
So, the hare sat down and had a snooze.
The tortoise, meanwhile, walked on at a steady pace.
He noticed the animals cheering him on along the way and smiled at them.
As he approached the finish line, all the animals cheered so loudly that
they woke the hare. Startled, the hare began to run, but it was too late.
The tortoise had won the race and the hearts of all the animals.*

## Instructions:

1. Look at the tortoise and hare continuum below. Mark an x on the line somewhere in between them to indicate where you most often find yourself. Are you generally more 'hare' or 'tortoise' in your life/work?

2. What is the impact of this on your physical body? For example, does being in this place often leaves you tired and stressed, or feeling like life is hard work? Or does it refuel you and give you energy?

3. Next consider how, where you are on the tortoise/hare continuum, impacts your emotional wellbeing. What are the feelings you most often experience? Are these feelings positive, neutral, or negative? Consider why this is.

4. How does where you are on the continuum impact on the quality of your thinking? For example, does it leave you needing to react to things with little time to make a wise decision? Or do you give yourself so much time to think that you often get lost in your own ideas, making tangible progress hard.

# 5 ADDITIONAL ACTIVITIES TO DEEPEN INTERNAL CONNECTION

5. How does where you are on the continuum impact other people in your life, especially those you care about and love? This could be your partner, children, teammates, and collaborators. Where would you put some of them on the same continuum?

6. Finally consider how, being where you are on the tortoise/hare continuum, impacts the results you're after at work, in your relationships and at home. For example, are you able to advance in your career as you wish? Are you making enough money? Are you able to give enough time to the people you say you love and care about? Or are things out of balance?

The key question is this:

> *Do I benefit or lose out from*
> *being mostly hare or mostly tortoise?*

Keep what works and tweak the rest

7. Think of some of the key activities in your life. Make a list to show activities that fit with the hare and those that reflect the tortoise within you according to the pace with which you normally approach them. For example, you may be a 'hare' when it comes to your sex life and a 'tortoise' when it comes to making any real relationship commitment. Don't attempt to list everything. Simply trust that what you list is what matters to you enough to explore this further.

8. Once you have completed your lists take a moment to consider both and reflect on whether some of the activities would benefit from being approached from the opposite perspectives. For example, you may find that whilst you normally read a bedtime

story to your child in 'hare' mode allowing you to return to that very important work email as quickly as possible you may, in fact, do better by adopting your inner 'tortoise' for the reading and applying your 'hare' to your work email.

9. Finally, pick one area or activity where conscious swapping or experimenting feels as though it could benefit you the most. Spend the next few days being mindful of this new approach and note the result.

Over the years of working with people, and also in my own life, I have discovered that often the more we want to bring our 'hare' to something, the wiser it is to deploy our 'tortoise' and vice versa. Whether it's a response that should wait until we're more level-headed ('hare' to 'tortoise') or 30 minutes of exercise or fresh air ('tortoise' to 'hare'), there is a time and place for both to benefit us.

Useful tip

One of the observations I often make for overactive 'hare' clients is that bringing more 'heart' to a task naturally slows us down.

This small tweak is often all that is required and all that is missing to do a better job, to connect more mindfully with others and to respond to life from an empowered place.

Paradoxically the more we rush the more we can battle with feelings of not having enough time, and the slower and more mindful we are, the more we manage to get done in less time.

There seems to be much wisdom and lots to be learned from Aesop's tale.

5 ADDITIONAL ACTIVITIES TO DEEPEN INTERNAL CONNECTION

## ACTIVITY 3: ENERGY CYLINDERS CHECK

**Goal:** to Connect with pleasure on a deeper level

**Time:** 10 minutes (or more)

**You will need:** mindful resolve to practice what can happen when energy flows.

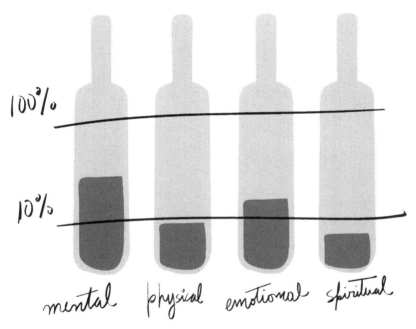

*"Before I knew it, my doubt and pessimism made me feel sad, my body felt like an elephant and my spirit seemed to have sunk into an abyss. And then I looked up above at the blue sky and heard the birds sing and my spirit lifted, my step quickened, my heart began to smile from the inside out and my mind found itself flooded with new ideas for what may be..." - Mary, coaching client*

## Context:

As we have seen, our mind, heart, body and spirit make up one system in which continuous energy-trades happen, without us necessarily being aware. When things are going well, our system is balanced with each part having enough energy to support us. However, as we put increasing pressure on the overall system to perform, we often force energy depletions. If you ever pushed yourself to work through the weekend or sacrificed a few nights of sleep to look after a sick child, you will immediately recognize this.

When our different energies are not given sufficient time to recharge, our system as a whole can become so depleted that there is nowhere left to borrow from. This is often what happens when people reach burnout!

## Instructions:

This exercise is an adopted version from my first book *Get Productive!* Practiced regularly, it will help you gain vital awareness of the energy you have to hand so that you are able to avoid depleting your reserves.

When you are at your best

1. Think about something specific you achieved which felt energizing and left you fully recharged. Something you completed in 'full flow'. It could be a dinner you prepared, a presentation you gave, or a successful interview that landed you your dream job!

Use the format below to indicate the level of energy that each of your four key parts - your mind, heart, body and spirit - contributed towards achieving this task.

*197*

# 5 ADDITIONAL ACTIVITIES TO DEEPEN INTERNAL CONNECTION

Mind % ____  Heart % ____  Body % ____  Spirit % ____

When things are less than ideal

2. Look back at something you did that did not turn out as well as you had wished. Again, note the energy that each part of you brought to this undertaking. For example, you may have tried to run a half-marathon, but the night before the race your partner broke up with you. At the starting line you felt sluggish and emotionally dejected but chose to run anyway, in part to forget the pain of your separation. It is easy to understand how, in such circumstances, it is very likely that none of the four parts of you would be working at 100 per cent.

Mind % ____  Heart % ____  Body % ____  Spirit % ____

How you are right now

3. Turn your attention to the present moment and score yourself (between 0 and 100 per cent) to give an indication of your current energy levels.

Mind % ____  Heart % ____  Body % ____  Spirit % ____

4. Now consider something you actually need to achieve or complete very soon. Given your present energy levels, are you up to the task? You may wish to ask your mind, heart, body and spirit in turn, relying on your felt-sense to respond. If the answer is yes, then your energy levels will support you through your upcoming task. If the answer is that you don't feel you have sufficient energy levels, notice what is missing. This will often surface key insight into what you need or how you can resource yourself to be able to do what you want or need.

Useful tip

Whilst it can be tempting to push through and simply force your whole being to comply and get something done, my experience shows that, over time, this can actually be counter productive.

We create the best results when we flow with a task. In other words when our thoughts, emotions, physical stamina and how what we do connects with our larger purpose or spirit align.

When we have to force ourselves, or some of these parts, to do something counter to this, we suffer, drain our resources and experience stress.

Preserving our integrity with ourselves (mind, heart, body and spirit) helps us make sound decisions, take action at the right time and generally do a better job.

Avoiding inner conflict helps us remain far more energized. And, with time, we will often find that our overall productivity and enjoyment levels for life and all our activities grow.

This can be true for you as well.

5 ADDITIONAL ACTIVITIES TO DEEPEN INTERNAL CONNECTION

## ACTIVITY 4: RETURN HOME

**Goal:** to align your internal energy enabling you to act from a place of true strength and power.

**Time:** 20 minutes

**You will need:** undisturbed time alone

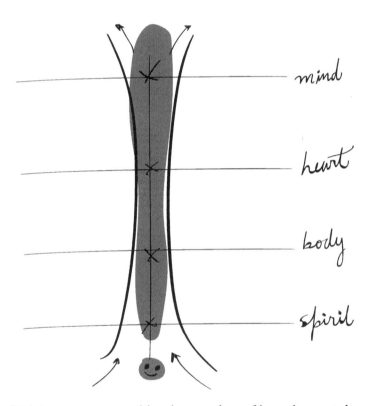

*"Life is not measured by the number of breaths we take,
but by the moments that take our breath away"*
Unknown

We all have 24 hours in every day and 7 days in each week. How we choose to spend the time we have resides with us. Life is a constant invitation to practice personal responsibility for nurturing oneself. Oddly, the area that is often most neglected is that of self-care. Looking after ourselves however, is vital for wellbeing and self-renewal. There can be no sustainable healthy creation without a healthy creator. Take a moment to think about an activity you enjoy that simply feeds your soul: perhaps it is riding a bike at full speed, or mastering a new yoga move. These are all small acts of self-care.

The following exercise will help boost your level of personal strength and resilience through vital attention and corrective self-care. This will help restore your alignment and balance.

Begin by imagining that your mind, heart, body and spirit sit on a vertical line around which your physical presence is oriented [see the drawing on the previous page]. This portrays you as grounded, standing strongly on both feet, feeling resourceful, emotionally open and agile – the 'integrated' you.

Imagine that each of your four parts – mind, heart, body and spirit – has a horizontal line running through it as shown below. To the

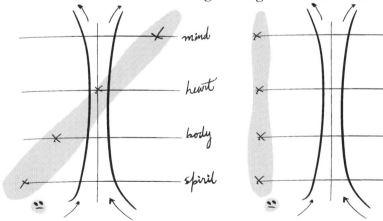

right of the center is a line to designate over-activation and to the left of the center a state of under-activation.

Let me give you a couple of examples to make this clear.

Example 1

Imagine a person whose mind is in constant overdrive. It is constantly on.

As on the drawing (above, see previous point) we would put an x along the horizontal line that corresponds to their mind – we would probably place the x somewhere far to the right.

Now, imagine the same person telling you that they generally feel ok. Along the horizontal line that corresponds to the heart, we may indicate this by placing the x somewhere in the middle.

This individual also tells us that they feel incredibly tired a lot. They have trouble sleeping and struggle to embrace the start of each new day. To capture this information, we may put an x on the horizontal line corresponding to the body somewhere to the left. Remember the left indicates under activation where their body does not want to move much as it lacks energy.

Finally the person's overall assessment or concluding remark may be that they generally feel lost. To mark this in our framework, we may put an x on the spirit horizontal line far to the left.

Notice how scattered the x's are relative to one another. What the diagram will show is that while some parts are dragging behind, others – the mind in this case – is still yanking everything forward.

You may think to yourself "Ouch!"

Example 2

Imagine someone else doing the same exercise. This person starts with an admission that they feel severely depressed because their life seems to be collapsing around them. They may have lost their long-term partner or feel very unfulfilled in their life.

Further inquiry may reveal that they can't face their challenges, so if you were to plot where their mind is, the x may be far to the left.

The x for the heart will also likely be somewhere to the left as they report feeling depressed.

Because of the frequency of negative thoughts and feeling sad, their body feels drained of energy so that even getting out of bed is a major struggle. So the position of the x representing their body is also going to be far to the left.

Their whole sense of who they are, their spirit, is difficult to discern other than to say it's 'missing'. Plotting this on the diagram example above would mean that the x for the spirit would also be far to the left.

Notice how in this case even though all four parts are aligned vertically – they are roughly in the same position – they are also all far to the left and therefore under-activated. This combination will feel hugely disempowering for the person concerned. And yet, at some times in our lives we may all find ourselves in this situation.

Can you see how the most empowered place within the framework of mind, heart, body and spirit integration is the middle of each

## 5 ADDITIONAL ACTIVITIES TO DEEPEN INTERNAL CONNECTION

horizontal line? This place gives us the fullest capacity to experience and appreciate the meaning of highs and lows.

Your turn!

**Instructions:**

Draw a diagram similar to the example above in your journal and quickly plot where your mind, heart, body and spirit is in relation to the center 'at this moment in time'.

Accuracy is not needed here. If you find yourself thinking too much about where you may be your mind is over-analysing the whole thing so stop! Go with your first instinct. To start you may not feel this is completely accurate but you will start to trust it more.

Once you have your results consider how this way of being serves you and the goals you have set for yourself.

If the results show room for improvement, consider what you can do to bring any outliers closer towards alignment (the center). Trust that as you give your mind, heart, body and spirit the necessary attention and non-judgmental listening, you will quickly discover what is needed to help you return to a more aligned and integrated center – a place of true wellbeing.

Case Study

I once worked with a very generous client. She helped everyone and didn't like saying no to others. It made her feel good to help. However, there was a drawback to her generosity as it left her tired and having little time for herself. Being always pushed for time also denied her the time to do the things she enjoyed and which would help her refuel. Time passed and her acts of generosity wore her down, made her irritable, brought resentment into her heart and drained her physical energy until she ended up with major health issues. Despite receiving a clear warning from her doctor, her patterns of behaviour was difficult to change. She had grown accustomed to being this way!

After working together for a few months, I introduced her to the Return Home exercise to help her build awareness about what was draining her and what helped her feel centered and aligned inside. By simply taking notice of where her mind, heart, body and spirit were within this simple framework, my client began to take small auto-corrective actions.

When she returned to me for a follow-up session, the results were incredible. She arrived with a giant smile, feeling recharged in spite of having a tough work schedule. She proceeded to tell me how she learned to put herself first instead of deprioritising her needs as she did previously. The three key changes she implemented were:

1. Making time for self-care practices to recover physical stamina and give her mind a much-needed break.

2. Saying 'No' more often so that her heart did not built up resentments.

3. Doing something creative that fed her spirit and helped her mind do the sort of thinking she greatly enjoyed.

Using the exercise above, she noted that self-care was fantastic for her body. It helped it avoid getting too tired. Saying 'No' was good for her heart. It seemed that as she started to consider how saying 'Yes' to everything and everyone impacted her. Saying 'No' more often resulted in her heart thanking her for the love she was giving to herself. And doing something creative that she loved fed her spirit.

I share this story with you because I have seen many people make similar positive changes with the aid of this activity. I wish you the same.

BODY TALK

# ACTIVITY 5: AMPLIFYING BLISS

**Goal:** regular connection with life, greater pleasure and joy.

**Time:** 10 minutes plus

**You will need:** a mindful resolve to practice

*"Stop looking outside for scraps of pleasure or fulfilment,
for validation, security, or love - you have a treasure within that
is infinitely greater than anything the world can offer."*
Eckhart Tolle, author of *The Power of Now*

# 5 ADDITIONAL ACTIVITIES TO DEEPEN INTERNAL CONNECTION

Many people try to be lovable to others instead of loving and honoring themselves. Pressures to fit in and to get along 'just to keep the peace' can create inner turmoil. It can severely dampen the individual spirit, stop us from expressing our truths and make deep connection with others harder because we act from a place of fear instead of trust and love.

To truly connect with others, we need to learn to take pleasure in our own lives. When we achieve this, it shows. We can enchant others with our sense of joy, our wholehearted engagement in a task and with the satisfaction and glee we derive from life.

Ask yourself when was the last time you felt total rapture for the deliciousness of life? Imagine what you would look like and how you would act if you had a deep love affair with your life as it is now. Too often, people are trapped in the search for something different or 'better' and they miss the preciousness of the moment and the power it has to enchant. If you seek to lead, parent, love and be helpful, you can also enchant others by awakening them to delight in their life. The best way to achieve this is by modeling the practice.

Consider the following situation that demonstrates a subtle yet massive difference. A person returns home to their family after work and is begrudgingly thinking "Great…now I also have to cook for everyone!" Another person faced with the same tasks taps into the power of positive thinking and their thinking follows this track "Great, I'm home now and I am so lucky that I get to cook for the people I love."

Note the difference in how each person will feel and also what they will bring in terms of energy towards their task and the people around them.

Our lives hold an incredible potential for joy and delight if we reconnect with them fully instead of allowing our minds to focus on how they are sometimes less than perfect.

This exercise invites you to take your moments of rapture and do the following:

1. Dare to experience them even more fully.

2. If appropriate, share them with those you love.

3. Consider where else in your life you can seek pleasure.

4. Sow the feeling of pleasure to your other daily routines.

This exercise invites you to become more mindful of the things that bring you true pleasure, joy and contentment. It will help you experience positive feelings more fully and more regularly. Your mind, heart, body and spirit will thank you and people in your life will also benefit as well from your family, friends, work colleagues, clients and even strangers.

Whether it's painting your lips red, baking a cake, having an orgasm, creating your next artwork, or playing a game with the family, bring pleasure and joy to it. Dive into the experiences you find pleasurable with all your senses and with no apologies. Choose to bring reverence and 100% appreciation to what you do, the people in your life and watch the magic occur.

Take your time and savor the experience.

Park all the mental chatter that creeps in telling you that you 'should be doing something else to be productive!' Trust that you deserve to enjoy the moments in your life much more. The mind is a great helper and aider but unchecked it can also become a slave driver robbing us of fun, joy and play.

Focus on how good it feels to be alive and become aware of your mind, heart, body and spirit experiencing joy together.

Choose to experience 'the now' more fully and take responsibility for making it the best it can be!

Some people take drugs to reach that high, but the best highs are those we can create drug-free. When your body feels good, your mind will function better, your heart will dance with joy, and your spirit will shine out. This is bliss and this is available in every moment of your life, or at least, with practice, many more.

**Instructions:**

1. Consider last week, yesterday or earlier today for a moment. Consider what actually brought you pleasure?

2. Name what brought you pleasure.

3. Think about the value or essence this experience connected you with. Capture this feeling in your head and feel it fully.

4. Consider what more your mind, heart, body and spirit need to feel content and balanced. Make a conscious effort to create circumstances that deliver what you need. Dare to reconnect within.

5. If the experience that brought you pleasure involved other people, take the time to tell them what part they played in this and the impact they had on you and how you feel.

- What helped you feel good?

- What especially touched or delighted you?

Dare to reconnect with the world around you through your bliss and you will create more similar moments. As the saying goes, energy flows where attention goes.

Choose bliss and create it wherever you go.

# Becoming a Master of Practice

## The science of body-centered health is growing

Science increasingly reveals to us that our biochemistry – what happens within every cell of our body – impacts our health and our ability to self-repair. As a neuroscientist, I can no longer ignore the link between the nervous system and the immune system, how the composition of bacteria in the gut impacts mood and brain function or the way our thoughts and behavior can affect our genes.

Scientific evidence tells us two key things

1. The human organism is incredibly complex and comprised of many parts that impact upon each other and are impacted upon by everything else.

2. We are constantly changing and adapting in order to survive.

Positive psychology – the science of human flourishing – invites us to learn from those situations in which we thrive. Apps and personal monitoring devices together with advances in Artificial Intelligence make it increasingly possible to gather data and notice patterns around what aids us.

Here are my top ten tips for greater health, based on the integration of mind, heart, body and spirit. These are the tips that have made the biggest difference in both my clients' and my own life.

## My top 10 Tips for a better you

1. Take control of your health

Call it personal leadership at its finest. There is no better person to look after your health than you, because you know your body best. When you wake, you know whether you're feeling at your personal best. This is why practices such as Body Talking, when practiced regularly, are so useful. They establish a vital dialogue with the body.

Regular health checks, actively enquiring about the state of your health, helps assemble useful information on how you are right now and it will also reflect the effect of any interventions.

I encourage clients to find a way to measure what is key to their overall health. These parameters may include feelings of contentment, the quality of their skin and hair, their fitness levels, their BMI, heart function, memory, sugar levels, allergies, the state of their gut, the strength of their immune system and the quality of the sleep they get. The axiom 'know thyself' is as much, if not more, about the state of your health as a foundation for everything else, than anything else.

2. Get good quality sleep

Of all the things that can be done, getting quality sleep is one of the most fundamental means of healing the body and also detoxifying the mind. And yet, sleep is often the first thing people sacrifice when under pressure. This is a mistake well worth avoiding.

Sleep is deeply connected with mind and body health. For example, sleep deprivation has the same effect on your immune system as physical stress or illness. In 2013, researchers at the University of Rochester Medical Center (URMC) for Translational Neuromedicine, made another vital discovery about sleep. They found that during sleep the brain actually cleanses itself of harmful proteins that are toxic to nerve cells if they are allowed to accumulate.[18].

In addition to removing toxins, sleep helps us to understand and consolidate memories. During the day, we constantly have to pay attention and learn new information, saving this to a temporary storage area in the brain called the hippocampus. Dr Mathew Walker, a leading sleep researcher and author of *Why We Sleep*, has been able to demonstrate that during sleep these short-term memories are shifted into longer-term storage. In another study, he showed that napping improved the ability to learn by 20 per cent. In other words, sleep helps the brain restore its capacity to soak up new learning.[19] The current consensus in the field is that during non-rapid eye movement sleep (deep sleep), neurons in the hippocampus and the higher cortical regions begin to synchronise their activities and convert the short-term memories, experiences and learning into something more lasting.

I aim to get eight hours of sleep each night because my body feels most rested when I do. Given the research on sleep, I recommend the same to my clients. For those with sleeping difficulties, I recommend putting extra effort into creating a calm, welcoming and deeply restful place to sleep. Dim lighting, slightly cool bedroom, a soothing fragrance, luxurious feeling bed sheets all assist in providing the nervous system with the best possible chance to experience a deep level of comfort and safety through as many senses as possible. Whilst our individual circadian clocks (how our bodies keep a natural day/night rhythm) differ a great deal – think night owl or early bird – getting the right amount and type of sleep is invaluable. While some people

---

18    Lulu Xie et al. (2013). Sleep Drives Metabolite Clearance from the Adult Brain *Science* 342(6156): 373-377.
19    Matthew Walker. (2018) *Why We Sleep: the New Science of Sleep and Dreams.* London: Penguin Books.

truly struggle to achieve a good night of sleep, putting in the effort to understand your specific inner workings instead of following what others do may just help you gain better sleep after all.

3. A good diet

Information about the effect of food on our wellbeing is coming to light at an ever more rapid pace. For example, it is known that what we eat has a direct effect on our genes. Nutrition can switch genes 'on' or 'off', modifying risk factors for different diseases. Over the last decade research into the gut has been revolutionizing how we view and manipulate the delicate ecosystem of bacteria in our gastrointestinal tract. The specific composition of one person's bacteria differs depending on their state of physical health. What's more, the composition of the microbiome can affect mood and brain function. Changing the balance of bacteria in our bodies can change a whole profile of genes and pathology – at least in laboratory experiments.

While debates about what is and is not good for us regularly make the news, eating a well-balanced diet is highly recommended by the World Health Organisation, to protect the body against malnutrition and for the prevention of diseases such as diabetes, heart disease, stroke and cancer. As a diabetic, I focus mainly on reducing my sugar intake to help my condition. However, a low-sugar diet also has a positive effect on mood and energy levels. You will benefit from experimenting to arrive at a diet that serves you well in terms of how your body performs and how you feel both mentally and emotionally. I worked with a nutrition coach whose main advice to me whilst I tried different diets was the message that is at the heart of the book you're reading: "Listen to what your body tells you!"

What is good for one person may not be for another. Whilst science looks for regularities, our bodies are incredibly complex and unique.

The key indicator is how you feel in terms of vitality, strength, energy and mood over the short, medium and long-term. Look to these cues to see whether you're on the right track. So, whilst a doughnut and a fourth cup of coffee may be giving you the energy boost you need right now, sustaining the habit may well deliver serious health consequences later, something that you can simply avoid by having more knowledge about and love for your body.

4. Achieving a satisfying work-life balance

Set clear boundaries between your work and life. Avoid getting into a situation where work dominates your life, as with time and due to the power of habits, this will create a major imbalance that can be hard to correct. As I was developing my work-life balance model (which you can read about and try with the aid of my book the Get Productive Grid: a Simple and Proven Work-life Balance System to Help You Thrive) I noticed that work-life balance gets quickly skewed when we're not paying attention. One result of work-life imbalance can be a sense of isolation, which is one of the biggest hardships to endure in our seemingly ever more connected world.

To return to or to remain in balance, we need effective structures and disciplines to make small and precise changes that retrain the mind to avoid the shortcuts that momentarily feel good but don't sustain us. For example, one can feel momentarily 'happy' through retail therapy. However, if that same person has no meaningful life outside of work, they are less likely to leave work on time, as they have nothing to look forward to. Worse still, going home to an empty house with a lonely evening stretching ahead of them may even be distressing. Avoiding this and spending long evenings at the desk won't fix the imbalance but will, in fact, make it worse.

A life 'in-balance' fuels overall health because it feeds different aspects of our being. Making time for friends, connecting with others, true rest, cultivating hobbies and regular exercise are extremely important but not always easy to put into practice. However, the right approach, which I teach in my Grid framework, helps develop focus, creates better boundaries and ensures that work is completed without draining energy reserves.

Finally, I highly recommend making specific commitments about leaving work behind. For example, I conclude my work on Fridays at 17:00 sharp. However I work a long day on Monday because it is my creative day and I enjoy being immersed in my writing.

5. Regular exercise

Schedule regular movement and exercise into your day. According to Dr Mark Tarnopolsky, genetic metabolic neurologist, "the most effective therapy available to my patients right now is exercise."[20] "Exercise lowers the risk of heart disease, levels of inflammation in the body, the risk of certain cancers, diabetes and weak bones, not to mention supporting healthy brain function." [21]

I recommend that you experiment with different activities and find something you really enjoy. You may also want to find a gadget that helps prompt you to move such as a smart watch or a fitness band, or an old-fashioned sand hourglass.

6. Shape your environment to support your mental, emotional, physical and spiritual dimensions

---

20 Mandy Oaklander. (2016). The New Science of Exercise. *Time Magazine Health*.
21  Coco Ballantyne. (2009). Does Exercise Really Make You Healthier? *Scientific American*, https://www.scientificamerican.com/article/does-exercise-really-make/

Everything we perceive in our external environment arrives into our awareness through our senses. For that reason, our environment is one of the most important determinants of results, along with our inherent genetic makeup.

I recommend shaping your home and workplace so that they are environments that empower and motivate you. For example, you may want to create a quiet corner, paint your room a favourite colour, add plants, burn candles or incense or display your most cherished memorabilia. How you organise and decorate your personal space affects your mood and can either support your productivity and well-being or impair it.

Surround yourself with positive people who challenge you and build your confidence and self-belief. Have a few friends who are not afraid to tell you things you may not wish to hear but do so for your own benefit and ensure you have plenty of friends who know how to laugh.

7. Heal any conflict between your mind, heart, body and spirit to achieve integration

In Eastern medicine, disease correlates with energy blockage. I have found that clients who are dissociated from their body, who are too driven by their overactive minds and can't switch off, fail to fully connect with life. Their experience of things is often reduced to being mostly cognitive.

Conflicts between each of the four dimensions (heart, mind, body and spirit) create polarities and centers of denseness that block or impede energy flow. This means that the intelligence of each of the four components is isolated and becomes 'blind' to what else is going on.

In contrast, a deeply connected or 'integrated' individual experiences unity. There is little or no internal conflict. My work shows that when we have a brilliant moment or feel in a state of flow that creates a good performance, the mind, heart, body and spirit align. Such integration is not a goal in itself, but an ongoing life process. One of our key duties as responsible adults is to become aware of our internal conflicts and to work on releasing them.

8. Find your inner compass

The more integrated we are, the more we are able to work from our intuitive center of power where our true wisdom resides – our inner compass. Connecting with our inner navigation systems can be done through regular meditation, mindfulness practices and simply coming into momentary pause or rest.

There is a great deal of power and beauty in such moments. Tuning into your thoughts, feelings, bodily sensations and values helps connect to all the essential aspects of who you are, so that what you do serves your 'whole' and not just one isolated aspect of you.

9. Find your purpose and joy and step fully in

Without purpose, there is no direction. Many people work so hard to find their purpose, not realizing that life has already given them one: to live and experience life in all its facets. Too often, we can be so wrapped up in resisting or fighting what is in front of us rather than working with it. We may allow the goals our mind chose to propel us forward often having to exert much more effort than would be otherwise required.

I am not saying that our fates are predetermined. What I advocate is that we place more attention on awakening to what the world needs from us at each moment. By paying attention to what's happening, what we attract and where we struggle, we hone in on our sense of self, our identity and our purpose. We begin to get to know ourselves better and how we function best.

Every person is beautifully unique and stands to make an invaluable contribution. The point of life is to keep growing and loving. As one of my favorite authors, Leo Buscaglia, writes: "Too often we underestimate the power of a touch, a smile, a kind word a listening ear, an honest compliment, or the smallest act of caring, all of which have a potential to turn a life around. It's overwhelming to consider the continuous opportunities there are to make our love felt."

10. Connect with others and find support

Throughout the animal kingdom an early sense of connection, to our parents or carers, and feelings of safety are fundamental to healthy brain development as well as being vital to our survival, health and wellbeing. We need stability, love and connection for focus, attention and healthy interaction. Feeling safe and connected to others helps us flourish and develop a positive growth mindset whereby we remain curious and willing to keep on learning.

The degree to which we remain with these early feelings of connection throughout our life affects how much we learn, how we perform, how we recover from setbacks and the degree to which we feel our life feels fulfilling. Hence, at any life stage - be it at school, in the way we parent, how we manage people, what we're like as a partner, how we collaborate and even how we do business - creating both trust and safety, translates to creating the best conditions for growth and success for all concerned.

Your brain needs care, safety and love to function well and so does your body. These same conditions help the body heal. I encourage you to invest in strengthening your communication skills and undertake as much personal development as you can. Through such investment you will get to know yourself in greater depth and develop a rich toolbox of relational skills. Being able to establish and nurture deep and lasting connections with those who matter will have a positive, and lasting, impact on your life.

Finally, I encourage you to take up a spiritual practice that helps you reconnect with a larger consciousness or totality in which you play an integral role. Regular spiritual practice calms the mind, expands the heart, centers the body, nurtures the spirit and is at the core of all religions.

One way to do this is by experiencing awe. Some of my favourite ways to do that include: immersing myself in and watching nature, locating and experiencing tranquillity, meditation, chanting or singing, guided visualisations, the creation and appreciation of art and/or music.

## Other Books by Magdalena

- *Get Productive! Boosting Your Productivity and Getting Things Done.* Dr Magdalena Bak-Maier (2012, ISBN-10: 0857083465, ISBN-13: 978-0857083463) available on Amazon as paperback and Kindle.

  Discover 36 simple and highly effective activities to help you save time and become more productive across your life, career and how you relate with others.

- *Get Productive Grid: A Simple and Proven Work-Life Balance System to Help You Thrive.* Dr Magdalena Bak-Maier 2015 (ISBN-10: 0993525202, ISBN-13: 978-0993525209) available on Amazon as paperback and Kindle.

  Learn a simple and highly effective tool for staying on top of your life, work, self-care and career that will help you do more and live more.

## Ways to stay connected, engaged and more involved

- Sign up to our mailing list at www.maketimecount.com

- For latest news and ideas about how you can put this work to use in your life or to share your own story visit www.maketimecount.com or email: info@maketimecount.com.

- You can find me through our social media channels:

  Twitter: maketimecountuk

  Facebook: https://www.facebook.com/drmagdalenabakmaier/

  Instagram: maketimecountglobal

  LinkedIn: https://www.linkedin.com/in/magdalenabakmaier/

- Share your practice with friends and colleagues. Invite them into it so you can share feedback and support each other.

- Join us at one of our Heart and Mind Connection Retreats or commission one for your community. www.maketimecount.com/retreats

- Learn with us online through one of our short courses www.maketimecount.com/events

- Become a more integrated leader with our signature online Da Vinci Programme, a 12-month integration journey designed to help you reconnect within and achieve more in life www.maketimecount.com/davinci

- Read my book *Get Productive! Boosting Your Productivity and Getting Things Done.* Dr Magdalena Bak-Maier (2012, ISBN-10: 0857083465, ISBN-13: 978-0857083463) available on Amazon and at www.maketimecount.com.

- Read my book *The Get Productive Grid: A Simple and Proven Work-Life Balance System to Help You Thrive.* Dr Magdalena Bak-Maier 2015 AVAILABLE WHERE? (ISBN-10: 0993525202, ISBN-13: 978-0993525209)

- Watch Magdalena's TEDx talk 2013 Let Your Heart Drive and Your Brain Lead the Way https://www.youtube.com/watch?v=sB-suIAscshE&t=3s

- Watch Magdalena's TEDx talk 2015 The incredible power of looking at the world with 'kind eyes' https://www.youtube.com/watch?v=HLt4rOJZa4w&t=16s

## Help us spread integration work

My work is dedicated to helping people discover the power of integration so they can rediscover their own power. This power is best felt when there is a unity of mind, heart, body and spirit. As inner conflict leaves, more becomes possible for the individual, their families, workplaces, and whole communities.

Internal conflict has a negative impact on the individual and how the world works and I'm committed to help transform it one heart and mind at a time.

You can support this work in the following ways:

- Help others discover this book by recommending it to them.

- Write a book review on Amazon or Goodreads.

- Invite a workshop or keynote into your organization, professional association or practitioner group.

- Recommend media people and podcast hosts to commission an interview with me.

We collaborate with institutions, researchers, fellow practitioners, creatives and artists. If you're interested in creating a collaborative project please drop us a line at info@maketimecount.com.

We love to hear from you.

Finally, if you'd like to join our team and believe you can help us with our mission please send an enquiry to info@maketimecount.com outlining your specific skills and interests and what you'd like to add to our team. We offer paid summer internships for recent graduates, and support part-time workers and people wanting to return to work.

# About

ABOUT

## Magdalena Bak-Maier

I am endlessly fascinated by how to help people find their true power and reconnect their mind, heart, body and spirit to feel empowered. My work draws on my PhD in Neuroscience from Caltech – California Institute of Technology, USA, as well as the original tools and systems I developed over the last two decades to help people connect within and perform at their very best. It also draws on the practical application of these approaches with one-to-one clients, fellow practitioners, in masterclasses, workshops, group programmes and on retreats. I integrate mind, heart, body and spirit through experiences and practical tools to help each individual to accept themselves as a resilient and powerful entity.

I've spent many years studying the miracle that is our nervous system: a giant network of nerve cells that allows us to experience the external world as well as what it feels like to be us and what powers our desire to go beyond mere survival. Today, the leading edge of my work is to understand how we create and develop a healthy identity and how we can use what the latest science reveals for personal development.

My own life experiences have helped me to value the power of the heart-mind connection, but my work has also drawn me towards the vital roles that the body and spirit play. When we become connected within, we discover peace; our lives become more 'on-purpose' and self-sabotage ends. We have a clear knowledge of who we are and a powerful set of tools with which to renew ourselves and step purposefully into the flow of life. I strive to live and model what I teach.

## What is integration?

I have developed a framework for achieving outstanding and sustainable performance that is also satisfying for the individual. The nervous system is our greatest ally. Working towards full integration is the primary way to achieve empowerment, not just for individuals but also for groups and institutions that want success.

What do I mean by 'integration'? It's all about the mind, heart, body and spirit connection. My hypothesis is simple: by enhancing how these four dimensions within us interact, we create optimal conditions for wellbeing and all facets of how we realize our full potential. This is 'integration' and it's the neuroscientific equivalent of a true superpower.

Integration can facilitate brilliance, joy and feeling 'whole'. Our challenge - and the basis of my pioneering approach - is to discover the tools and processes that help us align and connect within so we can lead empowered lives. The effort is worth it because when we're firing on all four cylinders - heart, mind, body, spirit - we can make positive

changes not only to our wellbeing, but to our productivity, workplace culture and even our global society.

Being connected within translates into greater authenticity, presence, confidence and fulfilment as we live out our values, and a healthy sense of personal agency. In the workplace, people who are integrated appear to have fewer issues; they are more productive and make better managers and leaders. Integration allows us to be more creative, innovative, resilient and agile and it fosters better teamwork.

It is time to reconnect within. When we integrate within we will live more fully, connect with each other more effectively and together co-create a better world.

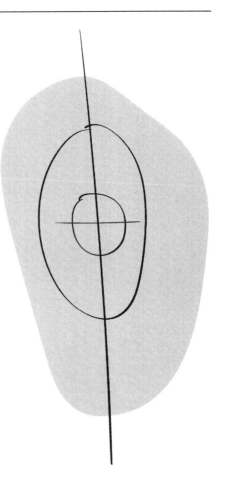

## How the work develops and who I share it with

Focusing on heart and mind connection has allowed me to demonstrate that, when people are nurtured and developed in this way, their performance soars, their local culture improves and the company/organisation in question wins in terms of brand perception. I have called this the 'triple benefit' of an integrative approach to fostering talent. When we are integrated we operate from a place of wellbeing that is sustainable.

At Imperial College London – a world leading research university – I designed and directed an experimental leadership programme focused on research, field and organizational leadership using the principles of integration. Since my original work at Imperial, I have repeated similar experiments in human empowerment at NOVA University in Portugal and at Koç University in Turkey, showing that when we focus on integration, the individual, the system and the institutional brand all benefit. I was awarded a Senior Fellowship by the UK Higher Education Academy in recognition of my work integrating neuroscience, coaching, leadership and education and I am delighted to say that fellow coaching practitioners and individuals from some of the most renowned institutions such as Columbia University, Stanford University, the Pasteur Institute, Max Planck Centers and the Royal College of Medicine have begun to embrace and adopt my approach.

To my delight my work has grown way beyond higher education. I've shared my tools and methods with the likes of NASA's senior leadership team, at the O2 Arena in London for the global AEG music and entertainment summit, staff at the New York Times and an international gathering of leaders across the United Nations Career Roundtables and many medical organizations. My Grid tool is now used by the internal Coaching Academy at Network Rail and many hundreds of practitioners, consultants and coaches.

## ABOUT

I've been a guest expert and speaker on BBC TV and Radio as well as many other key media outlets worldwide, including two dossiers on how integration can promote productivity, prevent burnout and enhance relationships for *Psychologies Magazine*. I've given two TEDx talks, (1) *Let Your Heart Drive and Your Brain Lead the Way*, viewed by over 17000 times, and (2) *The incredible power of looking at the world with 'kind eyes'* and written two productivity books; *Get Productive* and *The Get Productive Grid*.

My work keeps evolving. I was Life Coach of the Year Finalist (2015). In 2018, Getthegloss.com named me one of the Top 10 Inspirational Women in Wellbeing for bringing self-care into the main stream. I've given two British Psychological Society masterclasses (2015 and 2017), an invited workshop at the 2018 International Positive Psychology Conference in Hungary and I have served as Vice Chair for the Association of Integrative Coach and Therapy practitioners (AICTP) helping me understand where and how theory meets practice. The journey continues and I thank you for being part of it.

## Make Time Count

I founded Make Time Count Ltd (MTC) to empower individuals as well as forward-thinking leaders and organizations to reshape their life and work in a way that honors and celebrates the human spirit. MTC is a community and an organization of like-minded people. It is also a philosophy devoted to celebrating the human side of humans and to discovering the power of integration in our lives.

The most satisfying aspect of my work is being able to share what I'm discovering with those who are interested in doing better, irrespective of where they come from, their age, origin, economic status or profession. The simple act of you reading this book, for me, is success.

If you find that the content resonates with you and you'd like to explore further, I invite you to get involved at maketimecount.com.

The real world is my laboratory.

I work with people who recognize the following principles:

1. Human beings are not 'replaceable'. Every individual is a unique artist and a potential artisan whose core mission is to be of service and value to others.

2. Heart and mind are crucial partners, which guide individuals and the collective towards full realization. They are grounded in the physical body and become the main means of expression of the individuals' spirit.

3. The greatest suffering within a person comes when the heart and mind fail to align, when there is conflict between mind, heart, body and spirit and where this conflict is allowed to persist.

## ABOUT

4. To continuously evolve and lead deeply satisfying lives we must nurture our full-being and help others to nurture theirs.

5. Lasting transformation is only possible through conscious, regular practice of integration within and with each other.

For further details please visit http://www.maketimecount.com where you can also sign up to our mailing list, see what we do and join us.

# ACKNOWLEDGEMENTS

For the underpinnings to my work and this book in particular I'd like to thank two very special, early career science mentors: Efrain Azmitia at New York University and Costa Dobrenis at Albert Einstein Medical School. While our life paths crossed before my graduate work, their genuine curiosity and love of investigating natural phenomena gave me a great, tangible model for how to follow my own curiosity. With each year, I see the gift of their mentorship as the best gift I got over that time and one I enjoy repaying mentoring others.

ABOUT

What I learnt from them gave me the confidence to go for a doctorate in neuroscience at Caltech. Much later it gave me the necessary courage to use the science behind the human mind to develop my very unique and creative approach to integration. In this way I have been able to continue to explore what best supports human empowerment and healing, as coach-therapist.

From the psychological aspect, my work has benefited tremendously from meeting Professor Tatiana Bachkirova. It was at her masterclass on developmental coaching and how to work with self that she made a reference to the focusing work of Eugene Gendlin. It felt immediately familiar to me in terms of understanding why the Body Talk worked. Development of my Body Talk method also greatly benefited from my training in Neuro Linguistic Programming (NLP) with Richard Bantler. As a neuroscientist, attending this training gave me the practical know-how behind many of the brain phenomena I understood theoretically. NLP is grounded in paying attention to the senses as powerful reporters of our internal state and the body is one giant source of this. I am also incredibly thankful to the work of, and training in, Complete Resource Management (CMR) from Lisa Schwarz and the work and writings of Peter Levine, Daniel Siegel, Bassel van der Kolk and Stephen Porges.

I'm also very thankful to the Arbinger Programme and my two wise teachers Sharon Eakes and Nancy Smith. It was in completing my conflict resolution and Arbinger coach training that I started to seriously think about the flip side to being in relationships with others. This led me to deeply contemplate what it means to be 'in a relationship with oneself'. Applying this thinking to my already established Body Talk practice deepened and matured my thinking. And lastly, I have greatly benefited from systems work especially as described by Richard Schwartz in terms of internal parts, Bert Hellinger in terms of general principles on energetic relationships and entanglements and Stephen Housner in terms of how these ideas are applied towards health and illness.

And while it may seem odd, I am also extremely thankful to my body. It has been, and remains, a powerful teacher for me. Here I'm also very thankful to the London YMCA Five-Body-Rhythm class that helped me and some of my clients connect with our bodies through dance, and a number of yoga teachers over the years. In particular I'd like to acknowledge the anusara yoga teachings with John Friend. His dance of the Yes and No remains part of my yoga practice and has been part of it since the 1990s.

I would also like to thank a truly talented integrative counselor and dear friend Jill Hough. Jill has, without fail, encouraged me in developing my work, trusting my instincts and the process. Similarly, much gratitude goes to my long-time coach Antony Perry. Our lengthy collaboration has aided my development across many dimensions but especially as a practitioner with integrity to follow and live my work. I am also deeply indebted to my coaching supervisor Nick Cromwell. His ability to remain open-minded, curious and to invite me into powerful self-reflection have been incredibly useful to my development as a practitioner where I often find myself on the edge of practice where coaching and therapy mix.

In terms of developing and sharing my Body Talk work a special thanks goes to the leadership teams of the London Coaching Group, especially Maria Hemming, Bob Griffiths and Kish Modasia, and now Jan Morgan, Carolyn Hartwig, and Trish Dooley. This well-established coach gathering gave me a very warm welcome in the beginning of my coaching career and they continue to support my work with invitations to contribute and share what I discover with fellow practitioners and the public. I would similarly like to thank the Kingston Coaching Group led by Roy Lane and Deborah Stevenson who introduced me to this circle. I have made several great friendships through this community. I also would like to thank the Richmond NLP practitioners group led by Henrietta Laitt. Whilst this is a recent discovery for me, my thinking and practice is deeply enriched through their monthly speakers.

A special thank you also goes to all my 1:1 clients. Your trust and willingness to explore yourself deeply with me has created an ongoing testing ground for seeing what works, how and why. Similar thanks in connection with my Body Talk work goes to all our heart and mind integration retreat attendees. It is here that we have tested many of the exercises in this book as whole sequences and have witnessed the positive and lasting changes we continue to see from those who come and return again. It is a testament to the effectiveness of these practices. I am also greatly indebted to many fellow professionals and practitioners for recommending my work to others and also encouraging me to share my work in different communities. Here a special mention goes to AICTP - Association of Coaching and Therapy Practitioners - who welcomed me into their ranks and where I ended up serving as Vice-Chair. Being exposed to fellow integrative practitioners has been wonderful for helping me see that this work is truly at the leading edge of practice. Thank you in particular for the warm-hearted and genuine support and gift of friendship from Mark Farrell, Myriam Ferreira and Yannick Jacob.

I'd like to give special thanks to my colleague and friend Kathleen Sullivan a fellow practitioner and wonderful human being and Ariana Jordan whose generous and public support for the power of the integrative work I do felt deeply touching.

I have placed this writing project in the hands of my very capable editor and professional yoga instructor Victoria Woodward. Victoria's uncanny way of helping me find the words and lift my skills as a writer with each of our projects to new heights is fantastic. I'd also like to thank my personal assistant Sarah Adams for careful edits and proofreading of my writing in general and her overall support. Ozden Sahin who volunteered her academic services to this project has my eternal gratitude for carrying out the final proofreading. A massive thanks also goes to other members of my team for their contributions: Kyle Newman, Shan Houghs, Madeline Christey and Nikolas Melo. What you have brought and taught me in our work time together has been invaluable. Finally thank you to Meagan Adele Lopez and Chris Vika for giving me very useful and constructive reader feedback on early drafts of this book.

As an independent author and publisher, much gratitude and heartfelt appreciation go to all the institutions and specific individuals who supported my work as an organizational consultant, advisor, coach and talent developer. While there are too many to mention, I would like to highlight Peter Cawley and Peter Haynes at Imperial College London, Joan Crespo and Antonio Rendas at NOVA Portugal, Rui Costa at Columbia University, NYC, Monica Bettencourt-Dias at the Gulbenkian Science Institute, and Emrah Göker at Koc University in Turkey, and Ana Costa Freitas at Evora University. I'd also like to thank Kirstie Loveridge at AEG. To this list I'd like to also add my friend and colleague Vanessa Martin who after falling in love with my teachings has helped me connect with my Brazilian fans.

On the delivery front, I am deeply indebted to Carlos Vieira and his Ones Atelier for help with bringing our brand to life, the illustrations and the 'look' of our books. Similarly, a huge thank you goes to Stefan Maier who, with his mastery of publishing software and incredible generosity, helped me create this title in the way I want it to look. Thank you for your love and friendship.

## ABOUT

Finally, I owe much gratitude to my partner Marilyn Clarke. Thank you for putting up with my heavy workload and for giving me a safe space in your heart.

If you are still reading, I also thank you for buying and supporting my book. May its content serve you and all those whose lives you touch.

*"Be who you are
and
say what you feel,
because those who mind
don't matter,
and those who matter
don't mind."*

Bernard M. Baruch

Printed in Germany
by Amazon Distribution
GmbH, Leipzig